The Third Mandarin

Frank Kuppner was born in Glasgow in 1951. This is his eleventh Carcanet collection. The first, *A Bad Day for the Sung Dynasty*, was awarded a Scottish Arts Council Book award in 1984. *Second Best Moments in Chinese History* received the same award in 1997. A novelist as well as a poet, he received the McVitie's Prize for his fiction in 1995. He has been Writer in Residence at the universities of Edinburgh, Strathclyde and Glasgow.

FRANK KUPPNER

The Third Mandarin

CARCANET

First published in Great Britain in 2018 by
Carcanet Press Ltd
Alliance House, 30 Cross Street
Manchester M2 7AQ
www.carcanet.co.uk

A CIP catalogue record for this book is available from the British Library.
ISBN 978 1 784104 00 9

The publisher acknowledges financial assistance from Arts Council England.

Supported by
ARTS COUNCIL
ENGLAND

Typeset in England by XL Publishing Services, Exmouth

Contents

to Lavinia

Book One: Slowly Beginning to Gain Ground

1.
It is now very dark, but still they are by the waterfall,
Discussing the momentous problems of earthly existence.
Every so often, a third voice joins in their discussion.
They ignored it at first, but now they ignore it no longer.

2.
Crossing the bridge, he passes someone who, he is certain,
Was a fatal enemy of his in a former life but three.
The other stops, recognising in him a best friend from his previous
    existence but one.
Well now. Here's a challenge for their social etiquette indeed!

3.
Magnificent celebrations in the snow-roofed wineshop!
All three of the bright trio have triumphed in last week's crucial
    examinations
And have proved that they can recognise some half a million
    characters each.
The overweighted roof creaks. And creaks. And creaks. And creaks.

4. *A Letter from the Capital*
'Esteemed Sire, on my first day here I met three delightful fellows
At a modest, respectable inn, as a direct result of which
I'm afraid to say I have suffered a mild pecuniary embarrassment.
Do I perhaps have any relatives here who own two pairs of trousers?'

5. *Drinking Song*

'Why does every autumn feel like the final autumn?

Why does every spring feel like the first spring?

Faced by this more or less relentless temporal fluidity of quotidian existence,

I shall behave like any sensible person and go out and get royally pissed.'

6.

A small plank bridge crosses a narrow stream in the peaks –

As inconspicuous as a summer's memory

Of what winter is like. It is at present autumn.

The piece of torn clothing lying on it has been there since sometime last spring.

7.

If that bridge there were in the Western Capital,

Would the hound now happily embarked on it be in the capital too?

If so, I fear he would almost certainly

Not be wandering across it in quite such a nonchalant manner.

8.

The two officials leave the main building and hurry on down the road,

Chatting about what they had expected such success in life to be like.

As they reach the top of a stairway, they are passed by a featureless gentleman

Who was expected in the nearby palace rather earlier that morning.

9. *Drinking Song*

'For how many days of our lives, O friend, have we wandered thus by the lakes –

Over the bridges; across the streams; up sinuous hillside paths –

Exchanging our wise words about life and sharing our ever wiser silences?

What? Only a hundred and eleven of them? As many as that? Are you sure?'

10.

Of course, this pale, drawn, emaciated poet
Wandering calmly down a path through the forest
Will never write anything of the first importance. (Or, indeed, second.)
Hmm. He looks even more pleased with himself than usual today.

11.

Some scholars have gathered secretly in a clearing in the woods.
Nervously at first, but with ever-growing enthusiasm,
They begin to discuss the great, the ultimate problems of existence.
Those who think they are not really there slowly begin to lose
    ground.

12.

The road hurries eagerly on through the forest,
As though it were making its way in there for the first time.
There is nearly always something novel to discover every morning.
Those abandoned rags, for instance. (What a queer noise they are
    making!)

13.

At the height of summer, in a very small space
Between cooling rocks and trees, in an unfrequented
Part of the province, there sounds a complex noise,
Bespeaking simultaneous indulgence in two or three of life's greatest
    joys.

14. *To the Tune of: Late Whispers in the Twilight*
'Standing out on the balcony, near the crown of the pine-trees,
As the day after my ninety-second birthday passes,
I sigh to realise I shall never meet again
Those two vicious daughters of the neighbour who departed some
    forty-five years ago, alas.'

15.
She sits on the dark balcony for hours, admiring the view
Of clouds and moonlight flowing over the forests and distant peaks –
Until at length she becomes aware of an ugly noise in a neighbouring
    garden;
Somewhere among the flowers, but not quite a flowery sound.

16.
Ever since she found that note lobbed up onto her balcony, which said
That although, Madam, I am only a poor, retired scholar,
For years I have admired the subtle motion of your hips and buttocks
    from afar,
She has almost doubled the number of lessons she takes in certain of
    the key techniques of classical spear-throwing.

17.
Through the wall, he hears the voice of someone moaning in pain.
What should he do about it? Should he in fact do *anything*?
Outside, in the garden, it is clearly one of the first mornings of spring.
And there! – now it's stopped! (Hasn't it?) Hasn't it?

18.
Someone has just been stabbed in the lane beyond his garden!
But the scholar (no doubt misled by a common homonym)
Instead heard only the sound of some falling timber. (Odd.)
(Perhaps that's what they mean by living too close to language?)

19.
Late at night, wearily walking back home,
He hears from behind a closed window the angry cry:
'You think more of the Moon than of this old thing here, don't you?'
He turns off the road one lane later than usual.

20.

Two or three artisans hurry as best they can down the dark lane
Awkwardly carrying one large stone testicle each.
Oh, of course, the theory that the Buddha was essentially sexless
Has its fanatics! What great spiritual movement does not?

21.

He has been sitting there in his garden for an hour or two,
Meditating on the latest vexatious political instabilities,
When a shower of small jade balls scatter onto the lawn from the deep
    sky.
What? Can the Immortals themselves be falling out in awkward
    sympathy?

22.

After a few months, it at last occurred to him to investigate
The hollow base of the large statue of the Buddha he had lately bought.
He reached right in – and pulled out an ancient pair of something
    very like drawers.
An hour or two later, he returned – and reverentially put them back
    where he had got them.

23.

Pottering about in his garden on a pleasant summer's day,
He unearths what looks like a very valuable ancient necklace.
Something about it talks to him in living terms of dead love.
But he knew he had no idea what to reply.

24.

The old scholar stands astonished at a corner of his garden wall.
Since last he was there, years ago, the mosses and lichens
Have combined to imitate the most excitingly obscene character of
    them all!
How, he wonders, can he keep this knowledge hidden from his wife?

25.
The many petals which fell overnight from his prize chrysanthemums –
He discovers in the morning to be lying in mounds which suggest
The characters for *We Crave Your New Wife's Somewhat Exquisite
    Equivalent.*
By the next year, of course, these flowers are nowhere in sight.

26. *An Apology for Not Visiting*
'I did indeed approach your remote retreat to visit you;
There where, as you said in your letter, 'The plum-tree is my wife.'
But, on observing as I drew near that the phrase was, evidently, no
    mere metaphor,
I decided that the most prudent course open to me was to remove
    myself at once.'

27. *From a Letter of Condolence*
'Dear Sir, please accept these apologies for what must have seemed an
    unforgivably thoughtless remark.
The esteemed, sublime and able letter which you wrote to me recently
    about your late wife
Contained that modern tag which, I now learn, can mean either 'old,
    dried fish' or 'a sunlit cemetery'.
Oh, my friend! Never have I more regretted my lamentably uncertain
    touch with current linguistic nuance!'

28.
The scholar has been unable to continue his work this morning
On *The Fundamental Maturity of Most Chinese Poetry*
Because his wife has just beaten him senseless with the heavy
    manuscript –
Although, in fairness to her be it said, she did at least glance through
    it first.

29.

The pair of hanging scrolls at this table do not seem to be exactly
  matched.

One of them states: *Whatever life is, it is what this here is now.*

And the other: *My new wife's intimate household equipment is worth more
  than all the sacred mountains combined.*

Still, in the local pronunciation, they do at least rhyme. (Which is
  always something.)

30.

Now that the cruxes in the ancient calligraphic masterpiece

Have been fully interpreted to the scribe by a visiting master,

It has somehow, curiously, lost a great deal of its interest for him.

Again and again, he walks past it, unnoticing, carrying some woman
  or other.

31.

Still annoyed, the Prime Minister rolls up the immensely long scroll

Of border-post after border-post, city after city,

And places it precisely in a dark spot near the door,

Hoping his immature, sulking lover will trip over it on coming in.

32.

Noticing at last that the new neighbour's wife

Has a little, neat mouth and hard, glittering eyes,

The great moral thinker, rather to his own surprise,

Begins to visit next door much more often than he used to.

33.

The magistrate sits at comparative leisure in his large, radiant garden,

Surrounded by many documents and a few helpful daughters.

His neighbour's son can hardly sleep for thinking about the daughters.

The neighbour himself would much prefer to get his hands on the
  documents.

34.

No. That is not quite the sound of sandal on buttock.
It is, rather, the noise made when the great thinker discovers
That, of his five supposed children, only one is really his own.
And, she adds triumphantly, it's the one you like the least!

35.

This is again the day of that ancient, ill-understood festival
When scholars must kneel on porches with their buttocks in the air
While servant-girls belabour them with inferior copies of the classics.
Odd. One might have thought this would have died out long before
    now.

36.

Frowning again, the girl looked over from the table
On which she knelt with her tender little behind in the air, and asked:
'Are you quite sure this ritual really will release my Auntie's bonded
    soul from torment?'
From behind the embroidered screen nearby, a strong voice answered:
    'I am!'

37.

Of the line of elegant flowers which were nodding beside this stair,
There is now one less than were there at the start of the day.
Perhaps it stands resplendent on some poet's sunlit table?
Or perhaps the woman next door to him is wearing it in her hair?

38.

On the wall, a delightful picture of flowers.
On the table, a delightful vase of the same flowers.
A petal quivers, as if just about to fall.
It quivers again, as if still just about to fall.

39.
Dawn. A single candle burns on the table beside him.
For hours he has been searching through the Classics,
Chasing up here, there and everywhere a mysteriously elusive text.
Crucial? No. No; not at all. It is of next to no significance.

40. *A Political Allegory*
'In the morning, he is leaning on the table with his head in his hands.
Later, in the afternoon, he is leaning against a wall.
As evening begins to fall, he is leaning against a rail of some sort.
Now it is dark. What does he lean against now? Anything? Yes?'

41. *Opera Scene: 'The Shrinking Spy'*
'That candle has been shining there throughout the entire night.
Something important is certainly happening in our neighbour's villa.
Is it perhaps the hatching of a stray, nefarious plot?
What? No. On the whole, darling, I tend to think – probably not.'

42.
After a while, the candle splutters and goes out.
He is sitting awake at the desk, but he does nothing about it.
Soon, he begins to hear a noise outside, in the garden.
But, after a while – thank God! – it too seems to go away.

43.
A little pirouette of footprints on the path beyond his gate!
Leaving in the morning, he notices them and is baffled.
Was someone pacing up and down there, uncertain, during the night?
But, no. No – doubtless only some drunk, who couldn't even walk
    quite straight.

44.
Approached by one gate, this delightful and superbly appointed mansion
Seems to be the very epitome of enlightened, scholarly repose.
Whereas, approached by other other – but, no: wait a moment. No.
There *is* no other gate, is there? No. Oh, very well! Let's just go
    somewhere else.

45.
The great man, as he takes his last leave of the house,
Turns for a close, memorial look at the quiet garden
Where he spent so much time in recuperative meditation.
Ah – that magnificent view! It *has* always been there, has it?

46.
The small, quick stream tumbles modestly past an overgrown garden.
Over forty years ago, an important manuscript
Was thrown into it from this point, in a passing fit of pique.
Sometimes a thoughtful old gentleman pauses for a while on the path
    outside.

47.
Although the old scholar has lived in this retreat for some decades now,
The fact that a small, picturesque stream trickles into the lake
Just round the next promontory is still wholly unknown to him –
But then, his views on the real world always *were* somewhat opaque.

[*Alternative last line*:
But then, he thinks the entire physical world is merely a clever fake.
Vel:
Or such at least is the not unproblematic claim he likes to make.
Vel:
Or so he prefers to claim. (Perhaps on little more than a whim.)
Vel:
Or so he claims anyway. (A claim strangely hard to shake.)
Vel:

But perhaps this is all merely part of life's endless give-and-take?
Vel:
(And he'll be dead in an hour! Such a strange business, isn't it?)
(*Vel*:
Or do I perhaps mean, his brother?) (Yes – that's far more likely, isn't
    it?)
Vel:
(Or could I possibly be thinking of somewhere else?)
Vel:
(Yes. Or could I possibly be thinking of someone else?)
Vel:
(Or perhaps it isn't? Yes. Yes – I may be quite wrong about that.)
Vel:
(Or perhaps it isn't? But if not there, then where?)
Vel:
(Nor, for that matter, did he ever know who his *real* father was.)
(*Vel*:
So what on Earth does he think it is that is keeping him awake?)
Vel:
Or so he prefers to claim when he's wide awake.
Vel:
Even although, occasionally, it is part of what he might hear.
Vel:
(I dare say it would be different if he could swim.)
Vel:
(But, after all, what is knowledge? Or, for that matter, water?)]

48. *A Waning Folksong*
'This small stream is the boundary between two ancient kingdoms.
Does anybody still know that? I doubt if anyone does.
In which case, perhaps the suggestion here made is quite simply an
    error?
Yes. Yes – perhaps it was never really a boundary at all. Hmm. All
    right. Buzz, buzz, buzz.'

49.
The uncultivated wilds reveal yet another rude, glassy stream.
One would not have expected to find particularly much here.
Certainly that group of four drunks comes as rather a surprise.
(But no doubt the landscape hereabouts is absolutely full of such
    surprises?)

50.
The Zen poet, Chan Ce, is seated beneath a disused blockhouse,
Composing a fresh, lively immediate evocation of the ever-changing
    sunset —
When a dead body somehow falls with a thump onto the ground right
    beside him!
Of course, he then tries his best to work this detail spontaneously in.

51. *An Inscription*
'How beautiful the old fool's garden is in this uncanny evening light!
I feel as if I could take my ease here forever, behind this high, highly
    civilised trellis.
That stream would no doubt continue to run hither out of the
    distance, unimpeded.
Yes. Oh well. Still. I don't suppose I can stay here like this *all night*,
    can I, dear?'

52.
A man is standing on a bridge, listening to the trees above him.
Below him, the stream continues its casual descent.
In front of him lies an at best extremely hazardous future.
Behind him, a rock-face clambers indifferently on up towards the
    steep sky.

53. *A Political Allegory*

'The baffled man is still standing behind an ornamental rock.

No. That is definitely his instrument he is holding in one hand.

But who can say what the gently squeaking object is which he's
holding in the other?

Particularly since no-one else is awake at the present moment
anywhere in the immediate neighbourhood?'

54.

The silence of the broad, summery, afforested slope

Is broken by a sudden joyful cry of: 'Yes! I have a cock!'

Perhaps some nearby hermit (or farmer?) has at last attained
enlightenment?

Even so, the rock-strewn stream continues to saunter unimpressedly by.

55. *A Fairly Common Inscription*

'I sometimes wonder what right I have to enjoy myself quite so much
here

In this quiet, secluded retreat, with a fine view of waters and hills –

While elsewhere so many others must suffer cruelly from hardship
and overwork.

But then mature reflection inclines me to think: "Underwear!"'

56.

After thirty or so years sequestered in his quiet, leafy retreat,

The retired official wakens up on another safe, calm, promising
morning

And realises that, for a long time now, he has absolutely hated this
bloody tedious place.

He turns over on his side and, farting, tries to improve the national
anthem.

57.
Each day or so for years, the two ever fatter officials
Have met to discuss art, and the vital questions of existence,
In this noisy but elegant tea-room half-concealed in a quiet lane.
(All three have been told *at least once* to *never come back here again*.)

58.
The tiny, muddy stairway at the wineshop's outer wall
Leads down towards a dark, dismal, unpromising cellar.
And so very few people know that the landlord's outlawed cousin
Has been [*a two-character gap*] in here for the last twenty-odd years.

59. *Poem Written While Under the Influence*
'Beloved friend, at such an inspired early hour as this,
I remember the many good times we have seen together – almost –
And also the fact that you broke that favourite vase of mine thirteen
  years ago.
You did! You know you did! You absolute bastard! That's why I
  poisoned your wife! Er – I mean, your *horse* – sorry. Sorry.'

60.
If every fallen leaf here represented a human being
Whom he has seen mentioned in his official reports,
How many trees more or less would this forest need to have –
He wonders for a few seconds, before getting back onto his horse.

61. *Opera Scene: 'The Lo Man Actor'*
'Alas, because I was for a few years in my youth an actor,
I now find myself disqualified from seeking high official office –
And all this despite performing as some of the greatest men in history!
To widespread acclaim! They loved me! (Did *nobody* see my reviews?)'

62. *Inscribed Rather Low on a Public Wall*
'For forty years I ploughed the harsh fields of the inkslab,
A harmless official drudge – until a passing Madame
Asked me to lug a tub into a house for her one morning –
And suddenly I understood Fate from the inside.'

63. *His Epitaph for Himself*
'How fortunate I feel I am, to have been allowed to work here
In this small riverside town, safe in the world's only real country
For my whole life, some seventy-odd years of quiet productive
    mercantile drudgery.
Oh, if only my eight or nine sons could have been at least a *little* more
    like myself!'

64.
He sits on the terrace, looking out at the water,
As he has done every day for the last thirty-odd years,
Barring the occasional illness, or storm, or vital visit.
Once again, a small boat bobs at a far-off landing-place.

65.
The priest eventually emerges from his profound meditations, to
    discover
That some thief or other must have made surreptitiously off with his
    precious skiff!
Very well then! Fine! He shall just spend the rest of his entire life on
    this sacred island!
(And his small room in the town does indeed remain unentered for
    the next few days at least.)

66.
Quite as to why this charming uninhabited island
Is known as *The Meeting-Place of the Two Shy Triplets*
Local history does not relate, or seems to have forgotten.
But, look! Thin, rotting ropes still hang from some of the branches!

67.
At dawn, the clouds swiftly darkened and the rain fell in torrents.
(How often has that happened in all the history of China?)
And an official who was just then sniffing at his loved one's *bun*
   sneezed.
(Which must still keep us in the many thousands, I suppose.)

68.
Comfortably ensconced in his private study,
With, on the walls around him, a truly astonishing,
Unequalled collection of erotic and obscene snuff-boxes,
The old connoisseur smiles quietly in his sleep.

69.
The petals which fell overnight from his prize chrysanthemums,
He discovers in the morning to be lying in such a way
As to hint at the obvious character for *sniff*. He sighs again.
Will Heaven really never stop sending him all these bloody messages?

70.
The old flower-and-insect painting, with its hidden, ecstatic message,
Hangs on the walls of the house for decade after decade
Till the parents die, and the children age and vanish,
And a friend's son quietly takes it away and does not bring it back.

71. *A Message Scratched on a Wall*
'Arriving, after a long, tiring walk, at this pavilion near the ford,
I found some dregs and scraps – though you yourself had already gone –
No doubt to some other pavilion much higher up the slope.
But at least this gives me the chance to say: *I don't really like you much
   at all.*'

72.

A few leaves blow around on the high path.
Someone quickly walks down the lane below the bluff.
An hour goes past. A year? (Or a century? Hmm.) Are we in fact here?
And yet – where else should anyone really be?

73.

Some shattered fences lie in a gully.
A small path leads to a higher valley
In which a few scattered bones are lying. Right.
Now, go back to the fences and inspect them for a few minutes more,
    eh?

74.

It was simple. He set out from the house below,
Intending to climb to the high, preoccupied pavilion
As he had done innumerable times before.
But he never arrived there. No. Someone else arrived there instead.

75.

That small central pavilion has remained quite unvisited today.
You know, this must be the first time in nearly thirty-seven years
That no-one has been here at any moment between dawn and dusk.
    Hmm.
Has something *particularly* important perhaps been going on in the
    neighbourhood?

76. *A Faded Inscription*
'With luck, I shall fall asleep, drunk, here in this dank Jade Pavilion;
Die in a bloated dream, and never feel anything more.
So. Please do not wake me up, my friend, if I should begin to snore.
My friend. Yes. Or *not* my friend. Really – what does it matter?'

77.
The gay toper has been looking all day from this elegant pavilion,
Out to where, across the river, a farmer labours in his field.
He has shaken his head in admiration time without number by now.
Indeed, had he not just passed out, he might well *still* be shaking it.

78.
Soon afterwards, waking up and realising
That what he took to be a golden bow is in reality an old hoe,
The peasant shakes his head, gets to his feet
And crosses to some harsh fields, where he works away until night
    falls yet again.

79. *Questions of an Intelligent Traveller*
'Aren't these ridiculous mountains at least four or five times their
    necessary size?
What an utterly absurd backdrop for a pleasant little fishing-village!
How, for instance, can anyone nonchalantly go about his ordinary
    business here
Without glancing up every second minute at such a precariously
    raised sky? Eh? (Whereabouts is the local brothel here by the way?)'

80.
This arm of the mountain range proceeds no further.
A sheer cliff ends it without compunction.
Sky is there. And there. And there.
Grass is there too. Long, silent grass[es].

81.
An intense local shower falls on the mountain slope,
But nobody is there to notice it.
Water droplets descend irregularly from leaf to leaf,
Unlike the nearby army marching strictly forward, bathed in sunlight.

82.

An empty room stands in Cathay, in the sunlight.
(But at any moment there must be millions of those!)
(What then is so special about this particular room?
(Has somebody wonderful perhaps just left it? (*Yes. That might be the answer?*)))

83.

'Can I come out now?' the voice calls pleadingly.
But there is no reply. It calls again.
Still there is no reply. Have they perhaps gone away?
A few more contented shadows glide silently across the room.

84.

A shoulder rests lightly against a wall.
Space in this room is at a premium, among all these books.
A hand rests lightly against a head.
Yes! This never-to-be-forgotten secret moment!

85.

The corridor continues secretively on and on and on,
Far past the living quarters of the important people –
On to vague regions of storage, function and irrelevance
Where the few occupied rooms might contain a genius or two.

86. *Epitaph on a Genius Who Died Young*
When asked what it was like to be so incredibly gifted,
He smiled quietly and said, with delightful good humour:
'Oh well, you know, one has to be *somebody*, doesn't one?
Just think what it must be like to be one of these [rich] people!'

87.
From all over this great city I hear keen sounds of enjoyment,
The lonely poet writes, perfecting his calligraphy;
Improvising on the fine new paper he has lately managed to buy.
But none for me. Invitation, that is. WHY DO I EVEN BLOODY
    BOTHER? EH???

88.
Half a dozen palace officials in their different apartments
Are writing the phrase, *In my considered view*, more or less simultaneously,
At this particular moment, as the sunlight starts to break through.
(One of them at least is making a very grave mistake!)

89.
The official wakes up and frowns. Of course. Of course.
In this cramped, temporary accommodation
He is forced to sleep in a single bed with all three of his wives at once.
He sighs. All right. Whose hand is it at his throat *this* time?

90.
In fact, over the slow, unsteady course of the transfiguring, almost
    all-altering years,
Three people have died in separate bouts of sleep in this particular
    palace room –
While at least two others have expired in what might reasonably be
    called a much less *dignified* manner.
But this next suddenly arrived new pair here now hurry towards the
    big, faithful old bed anyway. (Will they *never* bloody learn?)

91.
It was when the Emperor's heir, a bleak, solemn lad of nine summers,
Was discovered to be spending much of his free time each day in a
    small temple-yard,
Passionately biting semi-poisonous spiders in half,
That the drift to the pathless interior really began to establish itself.

92.

'The Emperor's rather strange Uncle has returned!'
The news spreads quickly into every room of the Palace.
Soon, some brave ladies begin to appear up on their balconies,
Dressed to suggest a certain dignified tolerance for vulgar abuse.

93. *A Political Allegory*
'The long, freely hanging sleeves of the court ladies
Lightly touch their sides, then swing outwards
To float in the palace air; before returning
To caress them in a quintessentially untrustworthy manner.'

94.

In the moonlight, on one of the lesser palace balconies,
A court lady is trying to perform a stately, unburdened dance
For a legless peer in the darkness nearby, who is joyfully encouraging
    her.
But don't all those cries of 'Jug! Jugs! Jiggle!' perhaps risk alerting the
    guards?

95.

One of the new Court Ladies gasps and stiffens imperceptibly.
Doubtless through sheer ignorance, the visiting flute maestro
Has just embarked on a tune known back home as *The Swinging
    Huang of Spring.* Dear me!
Fortunately, however – um – no-one else seems to have noticed a thing.

96.

After the musicians have finished playing, there is a long pause.
The Emperor sits on for a while, with his eyes still closed, quite rapt.
While he does so, the Empress at last hurries back into her place,
    gently panting.
Truly a narrow escape! (There follows subdued by nonetheless
    heartfelt applause.)

97.
The old sage sits in the garden, listening to a group of women
Who are performing music for him, using all eight classical sounds:
Silk, bamboo, metal, stone, wood, leather, gourds and earthenware.
Yes! It was well worth giving up half his ancestral estate for this ...

98.
The old sage sits in the narrow garden, listening to a group of women
Who are performing music for him, this time using nine sounds:
Silk, bamboo, metal, stone, wood, knees, leather, gourds and
    earthenware.
Yes. Perhaps he is frowning mildly – but it's not at all from distaste.

99.
The old sage sits in the narrow garden, next to a group of women
Performing old-fashioned music for him, using all the classical forms:
They tear. They blow into. They drop. They lose. They elegantly eat
    from.
They smash. They scrape. They rub. They hit. They burst. They wear
    with aplomb.

100.
Those rude unpolished gutturals
On the other side of the suave wall!
Let us move a little deeper into the temple garden, darling
To where absolutely no-one will ever dare to disturb us.

Book Two: There Is Never A Reply

101.
'I who have spent some thirty years in such establishments as this
Am well-placed to inform you, which I do so now, of the central truth
Concerning the spiritual life, and so forth – which is that, to a quite
    extraordinary extent,
It is about separating bes— '

102. *Opera Scene: 'Whatever Happened to Him?'*
'This place has several unique, specialised words for the Truth.
Unfortunately, what it does not have is mere Truth itself.
I have frittered away forty years of my life here, chasing ravishing
    shadows.
Still. Better that than some other form of shadow, I suppose.'

103. *A Farewell Scribble*
'Thank you, Master, for decades of instruction and help.
It was me who stole your "secret hoard" (huh!) of foreign coins
    twenty years ago.
I am also one of your "ghosts". But I realised yesterday, at last,
That to understand everything would be, somehow, to miss the point.'

104. *Opera Scene: 'The Confused Lover'*
'Oh, help! Help! I am being kept in imprisonment here
By a dangerous old lecher! Please take this message to—
Oh, shit! It's too late! Bugger it! Here he comes now!
Forget it! Forget it! It doesn't matter. It's not important. (Help!)'

105. *A Cry for Help*
'Help! Hello? Help! I do not like being buried here!
Kindly disinter my corpse, and take it to a place
The geomantic conditions of which are superior to those of our
    present site! *Please!*
This misplaced non-existence is its own form of Hell, I can tell you!'

106. *Trying Out a New Brush*
'As a young man, I discussed such matters as politics and poetry
With many civilised arbiters, here in our peerless, leafy capital.
However, the sad fact is, I very soon got tired of all that.
Wine. Lies. Red Underwear. Cash. Coincidence. Et cetera. Twat.'

107.
After a few hours, the poet rises to his feel – er – to his *feet* – yes.
Whoops! He is unsteady. Much unsteadier than he had anticipated.
Now – which way is it back to the capital? What? The capital!
Let's see. Which capital? They changed it recently, didn't they?

108.
Out strolling, the poet glances across at a broken fence.
Instantly a brilliant metaphor forms in his mind
For much that recently happened to the Northern Pa Ling. Yes.
He'll write it down when back at home. Yes. He'll certainly
    remember it.

109. *An Exquisitely Written Inscription in a Viewing Pavilion*
'Why is this beautiful high roof here not more famous?
Why has this curious slim rock not been celebrated
By any of our highly distinguished poets and painters? Hmmm.
Let's see ... What else can I find to complain about—'

110.

The sensitive old poet is lying among a few bamboo roots,
Gazing in fascination at a small rock nearby.
This is surely the most impressive view in the entire province. No?
In fact, if he could move his legs, he would probably want to *worship* it.

111.

After four days of intense meditation
He opens his eyes again. Somewhat to his astonishment,
He discovers that his arms and legs are now variously tied together.
And what is this huge cascade that the raft is sweeping towards?

112.

The monk meditating beneath the famous old tree
At last reaches the deepest understanding of things (presumably) –
Just before the branch directly above him breaks off,
Strikes his head, and kills him. Him too. Yes. So, there we are …

113.

The head monk suddenly rises up into the air and disappears.
This is most unfortunate. Yes. Truly, most unfortunate.
Indeed, I can hardly over-emphasise just how unfortunate it is.
He's completely the wrong religion, just for a start.

114.

The summoned ghost touches his forehead, thinks,
Touches his nose, thinks, touches his mouth,
Thinks, opens his wine-jug, drinks, thinks,
Touches his eyelids, blinks – and shrinks back down to nothingness.

115.
A hum emerges from within the concourse of monks.
It slowly deepens and intensifies, until,
At an almost intolerable loudness, it suddenly breaks off.
One prefers to think of it as – the ultimate silence.

116.
As the soldier trudges up the mountain path, through a merciless squall,
He wonders for a moment what that strange noise is, so eerily like
The clapping and chanting of a thousand happy monks.
But then he turns a corner – and the path is clear yet again.

117.
Last night's gale at last removed the ancient, gnarled pine-tree from
    the cliff.
Then, later, it removed a substantial part of the cliff itself –
Including a slice of the old recluse's kitchen-garden.
But the pair who were out in it at the time escaped injury, thank God!

118.
A near-mountain of foliage surrounds the open door.
So much so, in fact, that the door itself is almost wholly obscured.
But that is presumably what the old man prefers.
(No. Don't bother going in. (He's not quite there at the moment.))

119.
The back door hangs precariously over the water.
There once was a rock path here, but it has been submerged.
Now there is only a door, which presumably no-one ever uses.
Still, I think we can hear someone preparing a meal nearby, can we not?

120.

The cul-de-sac path hugs the riverbank –
Coming to an end beside the door of a cottage.
Every few days a straying traveller might reach this point and curse.
Usually, he'll then retreat – though always with extreme reluctance.

121.

Just past the little bridge, the road splits abruptly into two.
A messenger is standing there, as he has been for some time now,
Trying to make up his mind which of the pair to follow;
Not knowing that, five minutes up ahead, they tranquilly re-unite.

122.

Nine or ten low houses cluster where two roads meet.
A deep pit is being hurriedly dug in front of a door
From which occasional long spurts of lurid, smoky flame shoot out
    – yes –
Just as if there *really were* some sort of supernatural prodigy inside it.

123. *A Topographical Note*

'This small road is a mere swamp of churned mud,
Though it leads to the abode of the greatest thinker who has lived
    hereabouts for centuries.
(I wonder what he is doing just at this moment?
(Not the usual nonsense with servant-girls, I very much hope.))'

124.

The road hurries on eagerly to the forest,
As if it were making its way in for the first time.
Yes. Nearly always something novel to be found there every morning.
Lost coins, for instance. Or blood. Yes. Or a wild riot of footprints.

125.
'This small road is a mere swamp of churned mud,
Though it leads to the abode of the greatest thinker who has lived
   hereabouts for centuries.
(You know, I *still* wonder what he might be doing just at this moment.)
(Oh, all right then. What he'll be doing once he's *finished* doing that.)'

126.
An elderly philosopher is walking by the river
In an isolated, gloomy, now very wet part of the city,
Using a profound insight into the innermost nature of Reality
To shelter himself as best he can from a merciless, switching
   downpour. (Best of luck!)

127. *An Inscription*
'Everyone else has staggered off because of the downpour –
But I remain seated here, half-sheltered beside the river,
Entranced by the shimmering, rippling impact of the rain.
Yes! Thank God for some decent and sober conversation at last!'

128.
A clump of trees provides the fortune-teller with shelter from the
   rainfall.
He should be late for his engagement by perhaps a few minutes. No
   more …
Or so it had certainly seemed. Yes. Yet – though the downpour ceased
   shortly afterwards –
He nonetheless somehow failed to reach his expected destination.

129.
What can he do but inspect the nearest stretch of road?
He shelters from the rain in a doorway beside the road.
How the – no! Wait a moment. No. Look! He just isn't there any more!
Let's see now. Five corners … Not to mention the door itself.

130. *A Political Allegory*
'Never before has the rain fallen so heavily
On every single day of the Summer Festival
As it did this year. But no-one is heard complaining.
For never before has the whole city been so more or less empty.'

131.
In the evening, the troubling rain is still falling.
Fighting continues in some of the finer districts of the city.
Yet, overall, the prospects are, one would have to say, fairly good –
With a much more settled *regime* due to arrive by the end of the
    week at the latest.

132.
The group of literary gents have argued for an hour or more about the
    subject for their next verse competition
In a favourite haunt beside the river, before one of them discovers
That two soldiers are lying dead in the surrounding undergrowth.
    Yes. Two *at least.*
With a loud cry of 'What are we waiting for!' – off they all go at speed.

133.
In a remote mountain hamlet, in a warm autumnal dusk,
A retired literary gentleman is standing, more or less nude,
On top of his garden wall, shouting: 'No! Never! It is just not enough!'
It is not clear who (if anyone) he might be addressing.

134.
The gifted malcontent who was caught inscribing an ancient character
Which signifies '*ugly, grim, obese*', or '*too fat even to stand*'
On a side-wall of the Governor's favourite summer-house, is thinking
As fast as he can. Yes. What room for manoeuvre has he left himself?

135.

A happy old fat God flounces into the river-village.
He dances ecstatically across the elegant bridge.
He jumps onto a well-wall – suffers a sudden spasm –
And, clutching his great heart, topples into the dark, unending chasm.

136. *Drinking Song (with Chorus)*
'So I said to the Emperor: Your Majesty, O Great Panjandrum of the
    Central Realms –
Intensely kind of you though it no doubt is of you to offer me
All your many daughters, wives, concubines, nieces, aunts, sisters-in-
    law, and so forth –
The fact is, I'm not that kind of man.' (*Chorus.*) 'Bend over, Fatso!'

137.

The recluse looks in astonishment at the messenger who has just
    arrived.
Not an hour ago, he was dreaming that the new Emperor was in love
    with him –
And here he is being urgently summoned to the palace for the first time!
Now – what the hell was the *rest* of that dream about?

138.

Several dozen potentates have long been gathered in the Great
    Courtyard.
What on Earth does the August Emperor think he is doing?
Well, it is fortunate that, at the moment, nobody can see him doing it –
Except, perhaps, for a couple of ladies, gazing enthralled through a
    keyhole.

139.

The Prime Minister wakes up, somewhat confused;
And, for a brief moment, he simply cannot remember
Why his private parts are chained to an expensive jade gong.
However – this is not the sort of thing one forgets for very long.

140.

The Governor is walking up a corridor
Which links (or so he assumes) his private apartments
With the rooms of a young enchantress he is particularly fond of.
He cries out as invisible fists begin to pummel his head.

141.

The Emperor is climbing a secret stairway
Which links (as he believes) his private summer apartments
With the rooms of a young lady he is particularly fond of.
But, at each step, one of his rubber tentacles squeaks a bit more. (Damn!)

142.

In a trembling voice, the Emperor begs the retired sage
Who is standing imperiously on the remote riverbank
Either to return with him and help him govern the troubled country
Or, at the very least, to let him have back some of his clothes.

143. *A Note of Explanation*

'When I called Your Excellency "a superannuated water buffalo",
I alluded, of course, to your utter indispensability
In the proper governance of this magnificent empire of ours. Yes.
I trust this also explains my (perhaps too brief) allusion to manure.'

144. *A Legal Verdict*

'Varlet, one final word before some bits of you are chopped off.
If someone did indeed inform you that the new District Governor
Likes to be referred to, perhaps joshingly, as *My Lady Limptool*,
He (or she) was probably only pretending to be your friend. Proceed!'

145. *An Epitaph*
'His penchant for (as humanely as possible) slicing off the noses
Of those he disliked, and feeding them to his beloved (and
    wonderfully rare) prize fish
Meant that an easy general popularity as such was hardly likely to be his.
Still. He was never one of those dunces who crave an easy general
    popularity.'

146.
Look! The ancient axe, specially constructed
For chopping the bodies of the worst criminals in half,
Hangs still on the wall of his little den, opposite him,
As he snores quietly beside his scowling concubine.

147.
He sits on in his quiet terrace. If he is lucky,
He will not notice what is floating past in the rivulet nearby.
It will drift away, and perhaps disturb a later, more observant citizen.
Yes – look! He's nodding off to sleep! (He has always been *so* fortunate!)

148. *Opera Chorus: 'The Great Leap Sideways'*
'Let us sit out on this fine terrace, making our great decisions,
As has been the practice here almost since time immemorial.
And if they cause the deaths of millions, then let us almost weep.
Yes. It's surely the least we can do, before we go back off to sleep.'

149.
The fat, old dog lies, apparently asleep, beneath the garden bench –
Wondering whether this is indeed the right moment at which to
    indicate
That it can see a cook creeping forward, with a drawn blade in his
    hand.
After all, it took him *years* to live down the last such mistake he made.

150.
The young dog stops in its tracks in the palace gardens,
Disconcerted by a noise drifting in from the distance.
Hmm. The last time it heard anything like that, the whole place
    needed rebuilding.
But it seems to be all right. Yes. That's a normal silence, isn't it?

151.
A dozen newly discovered caves full of distorted skeletons
In the underground recesses of the newly dug-up palace
Suggest to the more acute and diligent historians
The need to add at least a small conjectural footnote or two.

152.
A rather large skeleton is pacing about the monastery garden.
It refuses to say who it is, when asked. Indeed,
It will not give the slightest clue as to what its motives are.
Yet, it obviously understands the local *patois*, more or less.

153.
After seventeen years of searching, he at last finds the temple in
    question.
Yes. Yes, this is the place. This is where they'd agreed to meet!
He looks down behind a large boulder – and finds there a heap of
    mere bones?
Too late, it seems. Too late! But still: how *nice* to have been
    remembered …

154.
A hidden figure is throwing stones into the river
Over the back wall of a monastery.
An assiduous gardener, perhaps. Or perhaps a bored abbot?
It stops anyway, after some twenty minutes or so.

155.
Strange, to come back to the same sheltered, secluded valley;
To go so feelingly through the numberless sharp familiar details –
And then to find, in a clearing, that the great building is simply no
  longer there!
All those dark, interlinked decisions ... Where can they all have gone
  to?

156.
The cul-de-sac path hugs the riverbank –
Coming to an end beside a door to a cottage.
Every few weeks, a straying traveller reaches this point and curses.
A few poor fools even try the effect of knocking at the door.

157.
Someone else is walking along the river path now.
It is not the boy who appeared there roughly an hour ago,
Trembling slightly and sighing from untold joy.
No. This is much more the tread of some laughing fool seeking revenge.

158. *A Political Allegory*
'To be attacked by absolutely nothing is scarcely possible,
The man lying on the forest pathway at once concludes.
He drags himself to his feet, then stands, cautiously listening.
What? Can there really be *no* departing footsteps?'

159.
The path snakes down the mountain so circuitously –
One would hardly expect that, say, a wheel, a head, or a watermelon,
Released at the top, would follow it for very long.
No. It would soon run into one of the ditches at the side. (Wouldn't it?)

160.
Terrified at the thought of his continuing pursuit,
The boy runs among the trees by the river, raising an outcry;
Unaware that the strange man who approached him on the road
Has just been slowed down badly by having his head explode.

161.
A once pleasant morning has indeed deteriorated sharply.
The quack sits alone in his booth, tired and extremely wet.
He has every reason, poor chap, to feel profoundly upset.
He clenches a fist. He tries to replace his head. He continues to fret.

162.
Beyond the fact that he likes to have a bath three times a day,
To go out for long walks and return at inconvenient hours,
And prays to a head he keeps in a private cupboard,
They find little or nothing to complain of in their new lodger. (*Hooray!*)

163.
Smiling at the elegant daughter who has at last come back to visit him,
Somehow bringing with her a discontented, inelegant daughter of her
  own,
The fur merchant regales her with talk of idyllic incidents from her
  childhood.
Soon one of them is standing, slightly bemused, inside a small cupboard.

164. *Opera Scene: 'The Faded Scratch'*
'What do I do now, having reached the end of this spur?
I am reluctant, since I am not entirely covered by fur,
To vanish into the untracked wilds forever. Hopeless; hopeless.
Oh, how I wish the world's scene-shifter had not been quite so clever!'

165.
A few more weeds waving in a field.
A few cries from across the field.
Somewhere over there. Somewhere else over there.
Oh, the noise has long vanished, and yet the weeds wave on.

166.
In a thick mist, a pair of idiots have gone wandering down the lane.
Possibly they then vanish – and are never seen again?
Or, as is much more probable, somebody else will see them.
Yes. That is far likelier. Yes, yes. Almost *certain*, in fact.

167. *Excerpt from the Great Historian's Life-Work*
'On the last day of the following year, a palfrey,
Sauntering unattended down a lane between the palaces,
Was certainly seen by at least two or three gay layabouts
To hesitate for a moment beside a certain nondescript gate.'

168.
A tiny pirouette of footprints on the path outside his door.
Leaving for work in the morning, he notices them – and stops, baffled.
Has someone – timid, uncertain – been pacing up and down there
    during the night?
Well … no. Or at least, not yet.

169.
Cautiously, he slips out through an unguarded gate.
He hurries away exultantly from the magical nocturnal house.
What strange calmness in this lane! He thinks no-one else knows.
Never this utter joy again. No. No, never again.

170. *A Last Poem*

'Alack, just as I was so enjoying delusive timelessness near the Main
  Gate,

I collapsed here on this very spot and died – of a heart attack, I
  suppose –

Surviving only for long enough to scribble down these three brief
  lines. Yes. Yes.

I don't know about you, but I have great difficulty seeing how this
  could even be possible, Mate.'

171.

In a transport of utter joy at his unexpected pardon,

The old general throws himself to the ground as best he can

And starts to batter his forehead against the exquisite floor

To express his profound gratitude. (And there, alas, we must leave him.)

172. *Opera Scene: 'The Enemy General'*

'Perhaps his greatest joy would be to squall through a neighbouring
  house

Pretending to be a comparatively compassionate blast of thunder.

Even towards the end, when his health had quite collapsed (and no
  wonder!)

An unexpected fart of his could, somehow, be an inspiration to us all.'

173. *Opera Scene: 'The Double-Crossed Taoist Ghost'*

'Only on the day after your "Resurrection", Esteemed Master, did I
  learn

That you were in fact, whenever you had the chance, an almost
  frighteningly enthusiastic sexual deviant.

This, I must confess, now makes me view rather differently your
  advice on "how to live".

Yes. Particularly certain of those puzzling and difficult "advanced
  spiritual exercises" of yours.'

45

174.
A gap in the clouds seems to show a small gateway.
A gap in the gateway seems to show a small garden.
The newly dead child, who is sauntering through Paradise
Looking for company, at last begins to feel confident.

175.
Good Heavens! Some dozen Celestials are bent awkwardly over a
    barrier
Which runs through one of the secreter gardens of Paradise.
An inspection of intimate details by the Goddess of Purity, it seems.
H'm. No doubt she has recently been having one of her thrilling, if
    chaotic, dreams.

176. *Opera Scene: 'More Loose Talk In Paradise'*
'Oh, a mere flick of the Quintessence is all it takes that Deity
To have even his stateliest followers position themselves
In exactly the attitude he wishes them to adopt.' 'Hmm. You know,
To be honest, I'm slightly surprised that he still has *any* followers.'

177.
A few brave, noble beings, trying to escape from Paradise,
Are following an obscure and difficult path through a northerly
    wood.
Look! Look! Up ahead! There! A truly enormous wall!
Weeping with an abstract joy, they accelerate stealthily onwards.

178.
A Goddess with seven arms sits weeping outside the Great Temple.
She came down to earth, so young, eager and willing to help men –
But all they seem to want to do is talk about questions of sexual
    technique.
She wipes each tear away with a light sweep of a different hand.

179.
An insane richness of vegetation tumbles down the slope.
Lying among it, a free spirit looks up, laughing, at the clouds.
Who would ever have guessed that escape could be so so *easy*?
Yes. Only when he counts his arms and legs does he start to feel
    somewhat queasy.

180.
After thousands upon thousands of weary steps,
He at last sees the mountain-top temple right there in front of him.
He takes a few deep breaths, strips a membrane off (carefully!),
Swallows a final magic root, and stealthily crawls further on.

181.
Why is he waiting in the audience hall of the Temple
Wearing such a cold, strained, apprehensive expression?
Is someone perhaps being tortured there, in a sort of secret dungeon?
But, no – I dare say, not. No. That was only *a wild guess*.

182. *Opera Scene: 'The Two Solipsists'*
'How children come into existence is, I find, extremely odd.
One year they aren't there – and then, the next year, they are!
Then, after a while, they tend to age and disappear unexpectedly. H'm.
Am I really the only person who has ever existed properly?'

183. *From an Old Guide to the Province*
'There is something perverse about the very location of this pagoda.
One senses that its widespread reputation for illicit practices
Cannot be wholly undeserved. Visitors here are rare.
But if they don't leave instantly, they stay for many, many years.'

184.
After a highly regrettable incident of the previous month,
All the surviving attendants at the mountain temple
Have been provided with a large golden replica of a flea.
Though whether this will prove to be quite enough is still a moot
   point.

185. *Excerpt from 'A Drinkers Duet'*
'So great is the reverence for the word in this fair dump
That scraps of written-on paper here are never crudely destroyed.'
'No. Instead, they are carefully gathered up and taken to special
   hideaways
Where fastidiously trained priestesses wipe their immaculate arses
   with them. (*Prost!*)'

186. *A Commemorative Inscription*
'I came here to visit the tomb of the great artist – and at last found it.
And – very soon afterwards – I also found nearby, sheltered among a
   few trees,
This other, quieter tomb – of someone who doubtless deserved rather
   better.
Yes. It almost made me glad those young women had refused to come
   here with me.'

187.
'It seems to me that the thorny fields of literature
Are tilled to a disproportionate extent by sexual degenerates,'
Replied the Master, when asked why he himself had written nothing.
'Anyway, I am in fact sketching out a long sermon on the virtues of
   silence just at the moment.'

188.
Later on, when the Master has just left the room,
The dove flies out of one of his pictures and lands lightly on his desk.
'What a strange place!' it thinks. 'Yes. What is all this about?'
Then it eats some more of his pills, and escapes through the closed
  window.

189.
The non-existent bird wings its way out of the forest,
Feeling deliciously protected from the fields full of hunters.
Arrows sing past in the air, or thud against woods nearby. So; so.
How much safer this is than real life, it thinks, with a gratified sigh.

190. *A Political Allegory*
'The autumn leaves are in tumult all over the wrong, long garden.
They have watched the birds so often that perhaps they have grown
  envious?
They whirl around, singing a strange, not quite convincing song.
As if seeking a better life, they hammer at doors and windows.'

191. *And Another*
'The non-existent bird returns wearily to its nest.
It is finding increasing difficulty in locating a possible mate.
But it comforts itself with the thought that Fate is at least Fate.
Yes. True – Fate doesn't exist. H'm So they do have *that much* in
  common.'

192. *And Yet Another*
How terrible seems to him the plight of this poor, caged lark!
He buys it, opens the trap, and releases it out to freedom.
In its rush to escape, it flies straight up into his eyes, blinding him.
It falls to the ground. Dancing in pain, he stands on the bird,
  squashing it flat.

193. *Opera Scene: 'The Third Mandarin'*
With a painful grimace, the traveller, confronted by a tiger's tracks,
Shows he remembers his father, and his father's noble belief
That the wild beasts could be civilised by the soothing sound of
zither-music.
As the great cat dances towards him, he fells him without compunction.

194. *From a Somewhat Unexpected Letter Home*
'I am sure that no father ever wishes to learn that his favourite son –
Whose success in the capital by now seemed so assured, O My
Esteemed Sire! –
Is in fact awaiting public execution after a conviction for gross
indecency.
Thank God (as you so often remarked to me) nothing surprises you
these days.'

195.
As the astrologer hands over to the anxious parents the horoscope
which approves their tentative choice of a son-in-law,
An apparently distraught neighbour arrives – and informs them that
the young man in question
Has just been gaoled for persistently offering his august buttocks for
sale to deprived – er, no, sorry: to depraved – travellers near the
Temple of Miraculous Fertility.
The astrologer at once strikes his head, turns the chart upside-down,
and spontaneously hands back almost a third of his fee.

196.
The augurs take off their masks and gaze down enraptured
At the marks they have made on the sanded ground during their
blindfold dance.
How clearly it all reads: *This sad stuff is all so totally random.*
Right then! How would the unbelievers care to explain *this* one away?

197. *Village Scene*

The augur strides suspiciously towards the house of a neighbour
Who happens to be walking down a lane to visit another neighbour –
Who is even then strolling into the garden of a common friend –
Who is, at just that moment, grabbing the augur's third wife's rear end.

198.

Arriving in beaming haste at a cultivated friend's fine house,
With a scroll of a wonderful new poet he has just discovered,
He finds him lying in the garden, with a young tart spread all over his
      face.
Ah, Heaven! Yet more of this sad, sad modern indifference to rhyming!

199.

As they walk slowly among the trees, it occurs to them
That they might well never meet again in this disordered world.
And so, simultaneously, each turns to the other
To say what he really thinks of his dear friend's vast output of poetry.

200.

That's right. Kick the plants over and angrily leave
The small pavilion, vowing never again
To believe a single word that any woman ever says.
Then come back ten minutes later – you know – just in case.

Book Three: An Unusual Last Thing to Hear

201.
As they walk slowly among the trees, it occurs to them
That they might well never meet again in this disordered world.
Simultaneously they turn towards each other, as if
To speak. But they hesitate, say nothing, and stroll on.

202.
In the crowded street, a tenth-grade clerk sees a former teacher
    approaching him.
He moves a hand slightly, preparing a fairly affable welcome.
Nine steps, eight steps, seven steps. A waver. Six steps. Five.
(He should have done so much better!) No. NO! He strides unseeingly on.

203.
As the two scholarly colleagues are approaching their work-pavilion,
The first of them clutches his throat, totters, and collapses to the ground.
The second looks round, sees no-one – and runs smartly away.
Of course, one prefers to think he has gone to fetch help. Yes. Quite
    possibly.

204.
At last the curio-dealer's wife has laid out the staggeringly long
    landscape scroll
On the floor of the large, empty store-room. The old *connoisseur* rises;
And pursues her as best he still can while she strays up and down all
    over it –
Before finally collapsing, exhausted, in a lovely (if somewhat lonely)
    high valley.

205.
A long, long corridor runs along the entire length of the mansion;
And down the entire wall runs an extended scroll of landscape.
Numberless hills, valleys, rocks, pathways, cottages, stretches of water –
At noon, the owner may be here. Or here. Or, indeed, just
     conceivably, *here*.

206.
Strange, to come back to the very same hidden valley;
To go all the way through innumerable familiar details –
And then to find, in a clearing, that the great building is no longer
     there!
Perhaps one looks round for a few minutes? But, no – it really *has*
     vanished.

207.
A long, long corridor runs down the inner depth of the mansion;
And down the entire wall runs a long scroll of landscape.
Numberless hills, valleys, houses, rocks, pathways, stretches of water.
Slowly, a patch of sunlight runs across the wooden floor.

208. *A Very Striking Example of Dexterously Improvised Calligraphy*
'In these fine gaps between the rocks by the rapids
Are certain curious untouched cool niches
Which only the stoutest of us ever quite manage to reach.
Still: the great problem remains. How do we now get out?'

209.
Look there! A little grave in a forgotten valley.
Nobody need ever visit this deserted place.
And, indeed, no-one was at all near it for those few seconds
When a small voice drifted up, asking again for forgiveness.

210.

In an otherwise quite deserted border district
Three sappers are being out-argued by a sarcastic voice from a grave.
Yet another, it would seem, of these minor disputes over boundaries
Which can flare up at almost any time, for none too convincing a
    reason.

211.

They shall find him eventually, have no fear of that.
Granted, it is a high, dense, tortuous mountain –
But over a thousand soldiers are on it now, searching.
Yes. It is hard to see how they could possibly miss him again.

212. *Untitled*

'Once again, summer – and a listless, endless afternoon.
What am I doing here? What am I still doing here?
Surely no-one is doing anything at all this afternoon? No.
I sigh – and half a million soldiers nearby are nearly silent.'

213.

The retired scholar cools himself in his summer-house
With a delicate, painted fan – on which a young woman
Smilingly performs a questionable act in a chaste garden.
He turns his eyes back to his own garden – and tenderly sighs.

214.

Incensed, the great calligrapher dashes down a few choice words on a
    fan –
Then storms off without bothering to explain what it is he has just
    dared to suggest.
Cautiously, bemused scholars later pass the prized heirloom from hand
    to hand,
Each hoping very much he does not fully grasp it.

215.
Fifteen or so years later, he looks up and re-reads
The masterpiece of calligraphy above the door of his library.
Suddenly, he understands! He gives a conspiratorial laugh.
The next day, a friend arrives. Soon, he too is almost laughing.

216.
Twenty-three years later, he looks up and re-reads
The masterpiece of calligraphy above the door of his library.
Suddenly, he grasps something. He begins to frown.
A few minutes later, a servant arrives to remove it.

217.
The maid trips over a dark object lying behind the door;
Which either bites her, or merely imagines doing so –
Depending, this time, on whether it's a dog startled out of its sleep
Or the half-drunk brother of the city's second- or third-greatest
    animal-painter.

218. *The Latest Inscription on the Scroll*
'This calm view, so soothing to the anxious spirit ...
Staring out its consolation down the centuries!
Can the artist really have died, drunk, in a field?
Certainly the previous owner did. I know that for a fact.'

219.
A superb landscape scroll lies directly in front of him.
Only now, rather oddly, does he grasp its wonderful sweep and depth –
Though the picture has been here in his house for many a long year.
'Why have you stopped again?' asks a cold, irritated voice.

220.
She looks again at the calm picture of the calm landscape.
Suddenly, with a shriek of loathing, she tears it down from the wall.
At last! At last! At last! For how long has she wanted to do that?
'I must have been mad!' she screams – for nobody in particular.

221.
The *connoisseur* takes out, and regards with a thrill of pleasure,
What was once the least favourite picture in his entire collection.
However, that was before their latest, ferocious, domestic dispute.
Now the two little bite-marks – somehow – deliciously *enhance* all
    those tedious little houses.

222.
At dawn, the artist hurries into his study,
Urgently, he sets about trying to draw
The fiercest image of mature emotional frenzy of which he is capable.
Hmm ... That must have been *quite* some argument they had last night.

223.
The great general sits fretting in his favourite room –
A study adorned with several superb large vases.
You would hardly believe what there is inside one of those vases.
But ... well ... that's the sort of thing that happens in a war, I suppose.

224.
The retired scholar cools himself in his summer-house
With a delicate, painted fan – on which a young woman
Smilingly performs a questionable act in a chaste garden.
He turns his eyes back to his own garden – and sighs again.

225.
Having been separated for centuries,
The pair of vases has [have?] for a long while
Been in two neighbouring flats on either side of a city street.
And who has ever counted those who travel across this street?

226. *Suburban Folksong*
'The smiling matron languorously divests herself of her golden gown.
God knows why. A bath, maybe? I have better things to do with my
    time.
Or, if not better things, then other things to do at least. Hello.
I'm in that house over there, with the yellow vase in the window, by
    the way.'

227.
In search of a deep lane which had meant so much to him as a child,
He has got himself lost in a now unfamiliar district –
Which he had supposed he knew intimately. Strange. All too strange.
On the other hand, that chap over there does indeed look horribly
    familiar.

228. *Folksong From Yet Another Suburb*
'Hello. That's me in that house over there, with the light in the side-
    window.
To be quite honest, life has not been massively kind to me, has it?
But it's all right. I don't expect you to be interested. No.
Fact is, I'm no longer massively interested myself. (Just coming, dear!)'

229.
A line of some thirteen (?) geese in the sky over the river.
A shamefully exiled wit looking idly out of a window.
A line of four birds – a gap – a call – a line of five and five.
A question inside the house. Replies. Another small empty window.

230.
The river glides across the plain beneath a bolt of lightning.
A sea brightens above it as it flows towards the sea.
Earth? The earth seems nearly as untenantable as the sky.
Yet ten million people sleep (or should be sleeping) at the mouth of
    this estuary ...

231.
When he comes back to life, the boat is at least still floating.
For some reason, the sky has quite changed colour –
Though the previous hue seemed to him to be perfectly all right.
Yes. Why is there so much of the wrong light everywhere else?

232.
Emerging from the water, she climbs deftly into the sampan,
Picks up the nearby copy of a sacred text,
Sits down, makes himself comfortable [*sic*], and starts to read it. Yes.
Who knows? She might even learn something. *Anything* is possible!

233.
A small, rough wall has been built out into the water here;
No doubt enough to shelter nine or ten boats from any tumult
Which might affect some nearby part of the greatest river in that great
    land.
However, just at the moment, all the actual traffic is elsewhere.

234.
Within the waterside shops of the harbour
New numbers are fluttering on all the calendars –
But, quite obviously, it is exactly the same spring which has returned.
Yes. Indeed – many of *the same ships* seem to have returned too.

235.
The strange foreign ship which appeared down at the harbour
Has, it would seem, sailed off again without establishing contact.
Where it came from, and what it was doing both remain wholly unclear.
Can there *really* be something happening on another hemisphere?

236.
A somewhat higher wave than usual ripples into the bay.
Perhaps a large chunk of Japan has just disappeared underwater,
Muses the retired diplomat on the narrow path by the headland.
He snorts in mild amusement, pouts, then continues on his way.

237.
On these marshlands, the earth has had difficulty in fighting off the
    water.
As uneasy, scarcely respected truce has been declared.
Perhaps, an hour or so earlier this morning, say, a fleeing youth got
    lost here.
But now a distant bird, a light ripple, makes the only living sound.

238.
A few swaying shrubs; a few ripples of grass.
Three moderately high rocks are enough to define his garden –
In which he now lies down, at full length, with great difficulty,
For the first time in decades reliving a massive, shattering slip.

239.
Another mild evening. A dog lies quiet
In front of the small houses. A large rock – er, rook –
Detaches itself from the garden of a neighbour.
Oh, happiness! Happiness is still possible, is it? (It is! It is!)

240.

On a garden stretching down to a broad river
An old man lies, prone but alive, in front of the new Governor.
He may yet be forgiven. The outcome remains uncertain.
So much depends on whether the talking dog ever comes back!

241.

A mild evening. A hog lies quietly
In front of the small houses. A large rock
Drifts about the garden of a neighbour, crepitating.
What? What's that? Help! What is his eyesight doing now?

242.

Someone has just been stabbed in the lane beyond his garden!
But the scholar, doubtless confused by a vulgar idiom,
Instead hears only the sound of stoically falling timber.
He looks at the trees around him. Strange ... They are all so *horribly*
    calm.

243.

In the garden beside the large tree in the lane,
He has not yet quite emerged from a drunken stupor.
All this nonsense, he thinks to himself, has got to stop. Yes. Too old.
Too old ... Yes. And the jug not yet quite empty either!

244.

It is a moment somewhere between night and dawn.
He is lying in his garden, somewhere between
A dancing p[l]a[i]nt and a couple of dead drunk neighbours.
Such disappointing companions! (Except, of course, for the p[l]a[i]nt.)

245. *A Political Allegory*
Are these things old footprints locked in mud, he wonders,
As he lies face downwards, drunk, in his absent neighbour's garden.
But, in fact, there is a much simpler reason for the phenomenon.
As he discovers for himself, sadly, during the mating season.

246. *Opera Song: 'The Black Sheep of Bashang'*
'Ever since his elder daughter fell in love with a monkey,
It seems to me that our once terribly high and haughty neighbour
Has begun to steer his younger darling subtly in my direction.
(Which suggests that my disguise has – so far – managed to escape
    detection.)'

247. *A Variant*
'Ever since his elder daughter fell in love with a monkey,
It seems to me that our once ridiculously high and haughty neighbour
Has begun to steer his younger pearl subtly in my direction.
(Yes. He often sends me bananas as a special mark of affection.)'

248. *And a Further Variant*
'Ever since his elder daughter fell in love with a monkey,
It seems to me that our once excessively high and haughty neighbour
Has begun to steer his younger treasure subtly in my direction.
(Even to my incessant tree-climbing he raises no great objection.)'

249. *A Political Allegory*
Halfway up the garden wall, the exhausted official stops climbing.
He can go no further. No. No. It has at last defeated him.
He is old. That is the simple truth. Not even the encouragement
Of the kind neighbour on the other side enables him to continue.

250.
The old scholar stands flabbergasted at a corner of his garden wall.
Since last he was there, it seems, the mosses and lichens
Have re-combined and conspired to form the characters for *'Don't*
    blame me!'
Hmm. Might there somehow be an elusive intelligence behind
    Nature after all?

251.
The vital branch snaps, pitching him mercilessly down next to
His old neighbour's beautiful but likewise merciless young wife,
As she sits in their sun-drenched garden, directly on top of the overseer.
(The last thing he ever hears is certainly an unusual last thing to hear.)

252.
True, the branch which had been hung up above the lintel
To protect the small shrine from any evil influences
Fell down and killed the occultist as he was leaving the premises –
But what better way to die than for the things one really believes in?

253. *Inscription in a Viewing Pavilion*
'All round, becks and rills emerge from the foliage
Without ever quite gathering into a sizeable stream.
A fit of some indecision seems to have seized Nature here.
Good. I'd be perfectly happy if it went away and died of it.'

254. *Opera Song: 'The Chair of Zhuge Liang'*
'I very nearly died in this improbable clearing
Among high, gnarled trees, below improbable mountains.
It seemed utterly impossible to me as it was happening.
(As, to be quite honest, have most of the other things that happened
    to me.)'

255.
This single tree where he lies in the small clearing
Is at just about the opposite point of the earth
From a superb, light-filled amphitheatre
Where a few men with drawn swords are addressing a vast crowd.

256.
This small high bridge has been strengthened recently.
Perhaps an army will indeed have to cross it.
Unless the threat from beyond can be bought off
By the old chap at present having, alas, a crap behind one of those trees.

257.
One bank of the river here is so similar to the other!
He pauses halfway across the bridge, as near as he can manage it.
What an apt image, he thinks, for his entire life. Yes.
All I need do is fall off and the symbolism will be perfect.

258. *A Political Allegory*
'An army of blinded men is entering the capital;
Marching with uncanny precision, all things considered.
A strange depth of planning, obviously, has gone into this.
Look! Even the bridges are being effortlessly crossed!'

259. *Excerpt from a Ballad ('Of the Good Question')*
'The horses clatter over the bridge. Their riders
Gaze upwards, almost frightened, at the unbelievable sky.
Each of them is utterly prepared to die
For what they believe in – but why must the clouds so belittle them?'

260. *And a Later Excerpt*
'The small bridge in a dismal part of town
Has probably seen few days quite as dismal as this;
As over it passes a lengthy column of men
Each tied to the next by thick ropes. (What? Are you quite sure?)'

261.
Wild-eyed, sleepless, clothes flung on negligently –
He hurries over the bridge and goes in through the gateway.
Will he be too late to prevent a calamitous deed from happening?
Not so. (But – alas! – he will precipitate an even worse one.)

262.
What a lapse! They'll surely kill him! He races over the bridge,
Desperately trying to regain the safety of the poorer districts.
Is that guard still following him? Dear God! To have misused
The Emperor's own personal pronoun! A moment's inattention!
    That's all it takes!

263.
A young lady, wide-eyed, tightly grasps a bed-rail.
So? It makes really very little difference to *us*.
No. Rather, our gaze is monopolised by the gentleman
Who is hurrying across the bridge below, stoically weeping.

264.
Although once again this evening the sun routinely sets behind the
    hills,
There is no-one who has come out into this garden to observe it. No.
    Not today.
We do not even hear the hint of a distant weeping.
As far as we can tell, all the people in that house are, let us just say,
    sleeping.

265.

He plays his music again, for several hours each evening now.
He seems to have passed back to something like normality –
Artistically sending out banality after banality
Into a lane where, fortunately enough, usually no-one is passing.

266.

Dawn. More worrying sounds from inside the house.
Will everything be all right? Who can say for certain?
But it's all very normal. Yes. Something extremely normal.
The morning sun shall again light up a normal, quiet lane.

267.

The morning light takes its first hold on the garden.
Is this really how an ordinary day should begin?
Long silences, with bouts of mysterious scuffling.
Clearly, that can't be the light itself which is scuffling? (*Clearly.*)

268.

An astonishing light shines all over the island.
An astonishing light shines differently all over the sea.
Sunrise is not quite sufficient to explain all this, is it?
Well … not what most people would mean by sunrise, certainly.

269.

The man who has almost reached the top of the high ridge
Is the same man who is strolling thoughtfully by a stream
As it nears a severe fall, not terribly far below.
Only one of them has been quite overwhelmed by the glorious sunrise.

270. *An Inscription Scribbled on a Door*
'How could I be better off in a palace than here?
I eat fine vegetables plucked or picked from my own garden.
A few steps leads me to a pool; a few more to a precipice.
A few more to ... well ... what does it matter exactly, *where to*? (Mind
    your own bloody business.)'

271.
The beautiful calligraphy on the wall of the great man's library,
Describing in glowing terms a sunrise over the Pearl River,
Also secretly contains the pet names of both the maids
Who once climbed up onto that small table below at the same time
    (years ago!).

272.
No-one ever properly understood quite why it was
That the suffering old man, when at last he was discovered
To be lying dead in his bed in the morning sunlight,
Was holding in his forearms a small, broken table-leg.

273.
The official wakes up and frowns. Ah, yes ... of course.
In this cramped, temporary accommodation
He is forced to sleep in a single bed with all three of his wives at once.
He sighs. If only he had one more hand! (Or had turned into an insect!)

274.
The official wakes up and frowns. Ah, yes ... of course. Of course.
In this cramped, temporary accommodation
He is forced to sleep in a single bed with all four of his wives at once.
He frowns again. That particular hand seems strangely unfamiliar.

275.

A near-mountain of foliage surrounds the open door.
So much so, in fact, that the door itself is almost wholly obscured.
But that is presumably what the old man prefers.
(No. Don't bother going in. (At the moment, he's in Korea!))

276.

The official wakes up and frowns. Ah, yes … of course. Of course. Of
    course.
In this cramped, temporary accommodation
He is forced to sleep in a single bed with all three of his wives at once.
He sighs again. Really … why did he not file a proper complaint last
    year either?

277.

The old official picks up from his desk a small, neat box
Containing some hair ornaments given to him by women
Whose very existences never approached to within a day's journey of
    each other.
Ah, distances! Distances! Distances! Yes! What is more helpful than
    distances?

278. *A Political Allegory*

'A mingled sense of exaltation and failure
Ripples within the court matron, whose duty it was to ensure
That the Emperor's oddest son did not shock the young blades of the
    palace
As he carries her eagerly up and up towards the attic rooms.'

279.
In the moonlight, on one of the lesser palace balconies,
Several court ladies are performing a slow but uninhibited dance
For a figure in the shadows nearby, who is darkly encouraging them.
But at least everyone's motives here are pretty much what they ought
    to be.

280.
Five sisters stroll across a fine, private bridge together,
Talking and joking happily among themselves.
Each has recently been with a major court official
Who still sighs (or is one frowning?) as he thinks of her.

281.
Two trusted councillors ride magnificently away from that august
    audience,
Discussing what they'd at first imagined such immense social success
    would be like.
As they reach a bridge, they are passed by a profoundly distinguished-
    looking old gentleman
Who, several decades earlier, had been kicked out of the Summer
    Palace at least twice.

282.
The liar crossing the bridge finds it impossible to move.
It is simply not physically feasible for him to continue his journey.
Is this a judgement for some past inadequacy,
He wonders, as he waits for the situation to improve.

283.
The ageing rip sits in his garden, waiting for the group of paid women
Who are performing music for him (using all ten classical sonorities)
To reach another loud passage, so he may let pass a loud fart.
My God! But how one can suffer for other people's art ...

284.

The old mystic, strolling along by the sinuous stream, sighs.
How perfect it would be, he thinks, to die in a perfect place like this.
Yes. But what's that? Someone lurking over there in the concealed
    entrance near the new bridge?
It could be … Yes. Perhaps, on the whole, it would be safer to turn
    back home at once?

285. *Opera Scene: 'The Wrong Victim's Horoscope'*

'That nondescript gentleman walking across a bridge
Is perhaps unique. Unless we are misinformed,
He has never in his life suffered any personal misfortune whatsoever.
Right. You wait on this side of the stairs. I'll go across to the other.'

286. *A Political Allegory*

'Two heroes are fighting on that bridge over there.
And one would certainly like to know why two heroes are fighting
    on the bridge –
Did not a much more urgent question immediately arise.
Namely: which is the one whose face more strangely reflects the
    vermiculate skies?'

287. *And Another*

'Two men are walking over a bridge
Roughly carrying a bundle (not winter, obviously),
The weight of which is unequally distributed between them.
It squirms and moans beneath a sickening sun.'

288.

The monk carrying the sack discovers that the gate is locked!
Laboriously, he puts his burden back down onto the ground.
Whatever is inside it emits a weak, ambiguous sound.
Who could have foreseen that this gate too would be locked?

289.
He continues up the sacred mountain, carefully
Placing at every few paces on the path
A pretty severed tongue which he takes out of a sack.
Nothing matters in the slightest, except bringing the Goddess back.

290.
A meteorite crashes through the roof of the pavilion
And lands, very neatly, at the foot of the stone Buddha.
He looks down; then, obeying the whim of the moment,
He changes place and shape with it. (But, later, perhaps he changes his
    mind.)

291.
The queer owner explains why he opened his wine-shop just here.
He points to the mountains, the high snows, the health-giving
    atmosphere;
The uncanny light, the local womenfolk, deer, the living tradition of
    rhymed prose;
And the strange, silvery smoke which is seeping from one of his toes ...

292.
The man slumped, dreaming, in the small wine-shop
Is the same man as the one who is sitting opposite him, lost in thought.
At length, he reaches out, examines the sleeping head – and then,
With a smile of profound sympathy, he covers it with his new hat.

293.
He looks in astonishment at the messenger who has just arrived.
Last night he dreamt that the new Emperor was a depraved beast –
And now here he is being urgently summoned to the palace for the
    first time!
Immensely proud, he nonetheless escapes at once via the nearest
    balcony.

294.

Thanks to the fervent entreaties of the Emperor's youngest wife,

The spy from her homeland escapes being beheaded. Yes. Thanks to her,

He is merely whipped, branded, castrated, lashed to his horse, and driven peremptorily on his way.

It is not quite clear what his parting glance back at her is attempting to convey.

295.

When the Empress has the Minister of War brought to a secret room

Where she hands him a long, pliant bamboo cane – and demands to be soundly thrashed

To 'give [her] some rough idea of what our poor brave lads at the front must be going through',

He decides that another few days' delay in signing the peace treaty shouldn't hurt anyone *too* much.

296.

Secure behind her impregnable screen, the terrifying old Dowager

Has again chosen to expose her august self invisibly

Towards a newish court favourite – a wobbly-voiced advisor,

Who every day suspects he is about to be curtly sacked.

297.

The Emperor is hurrying down a tunnel

Which links, or so he thinks, his private apartments

With the rooms of a young lady he is particularly fond of.

For reasons best known to himself, he is dressed as a giant beaver.

298.
The Court Falconer wakes up, somewhat confused;
And, for a brief moment, he simply cannot remember
Why he is clinging to the roof-tiles, secured only by a leather thong.
But this is hardly the sort of thing one forgets for terribly long.

299.
With a surprising degree of dignity, the old ex-Prime Minister
Strolled into the hall and lifted his fine, aristocratic robes, to display
A wiry pair of bruised, gnarled buttocks – in what was either hopeless
    senility
Or a brave, symbolic message about conditions in the South-East.

300.
It's a day chock-full of ritual significance!
The Emperor in person drives the ceremonial plough –
While the Empress herself scatters the ceremonious seeds.
Lastly, the old Prime Minister rolls along [in?] a barrel of dung.

Book Four: Apart From You, Of Course

301. *Drinking Song (with Chorus)*
'What a yield! They didn't even have to fight for their autonomy.
No. All they needed to do was – cast a single vote for it.
And they couldn't even do that in sufficient numbers. Dear God!
No wonder I took to drink.' (*Chorus*) 'What? Weren't you a drunk
    already?'

302.
The quiet servant assiduously sweeps the courtyard
As he has done on perhaps a thousand previous mornings.
From a hidden balcony someone nonchalantly observes him
As has recently happened perhaps a dozen times by now.

303.
Yet another man sitting in another garden
In another city, with other invisible servants
Somewhere just out of sight in their other (less relaxed) lives.
No doubt he'll call them out when he needs them. In a minute or
    two, perhaps.

304.
Yes. A little grave in a forgotten valley.
Nobody need ever visit this deserted place.
And, indeed, no-one was at all near it for those few minutes
When a small, tired voice drifted up, pleading for a second chance.

305.

The blasted tree has been shakily preserved in the palace garden.
Long ago, the last emperor of a previous line was hanged from it.
But more than one of his successors has stood in front of it
For at least a few minutes. Then perhaps for a few minutes more.

306.

When sneeringly invited to respond, the humiliated minister,
In a terrible breach of court protocol, stood up, loosened his garb,
And urinated all over the still seated Chief Eunuch from head to foot.
Truly, a rare example of the heroic [final] piss.

307.

Behind the Empress's back, a woman is smiling broadly.
On the Empress's left, another woman suppresses a smirk.
Indeed, every woman in the room seems amused to a certain extent.
   Hm.
Has the Chief Eunuch perhaps been doing his so-called 'party trick'
   again?

308. *An Out-of-the-Way Inscription*

'The mists and mountains here are so well-suited to each other –
We feel like outsiders chancing to overhear
A wise ruler talking filth with his favourite concubine.
Which I must confess has long been rather a keen ambition of mine.'

309.

On Visiting My Aunt, the retired Imperial Concubine, Swaying Blossom,
At her charming Hillside Retreat, near the Pearl Breath of Spring Lake,
To congratulate her on reaching her 80th Birthday, and (alas!) finding her absent.
Shit!

310.

Within an hour, the appearance of the mountain had already started
 to change,
After the rumour sprang up among the hermits of Kangpang Hill
That an as yet undiscovered mixture of three local herbs could
 guarantee sexual potency.
Within a week, not a leaf remained – not even at the tops of the trees.

311. *A Political Allegory*

'Mist settles deeper and deeper on the small forest.
The leaves continue to flutter to the ground.
Wandering among those childhood trees, looking for his lost childhood,
Instead he finds only a decaying leg. (What? Here – just look at that!)'

312. *A Natural Scene*

Land visible among the wisps of mist.
A flood of water pours from a cleft.
A tree leans out insanely from a rock-face.
Oh, look! Those are somebody's clothes there, are they not?

313. *Traveller's Song*

'A thin gap opens in the mist – to reveal a gigantic waterfall!
Another cleft opens – to reveal a fine, unvisited road!
Look! All these fissures opening up everywhere around me ...
Nature, eh? No wonder I feel so comparatively at home in it ...'

314.

The wayfarer stops at the fork in the road, and looks back.
He remembers the promise he once made to his spiritual advisor.
He remembers the prostitute he recently saw, bending over a corpse.
Right. Now. Wasn't there something else he was supposed to be doing?

315.

What? Surely he has turned his donkey down the wrong road?
Or is he in fact just riding the wrong animal entirely?
Not so? Then perhaps he is simply the wrong person altogether?
Yes. That's probably it! (And is that why the road's so empty?)

316.

This somewhat conjectural marker claims to give the approximate
    point
At which the former territories of Chi, Wu, Wei, Chuai, Ying,
Kao, Yen, Lei, Ni, Ba, Da, Wun, Shang, Chen, Hui,
Liang, Hsu, Di, Wan and Gu all began. (Or, of course, ended.)

317.

One cannot help feeling that the proud ancient Kingdom of La,
Where all the coinage was minted in the shape of some private part or
    other,
Had a fundamentally joyful, questing attitude towards commercial
    transaction and exchange
Which is sadly lacking in today's more humdrum, materialistic world.
    No?

318.

Can that be someone on the distant road? But what does it matter
    anyway?
He returns to his reading. An absorbing historical compendium. Yes.
A superb discussion of former strife. A leisurely hour passes.
[Someone is just behind him now, quite unnoticed.]

319.

So, let us stand together here, at this ordinary street corner,
And try to identify which is the passer-by (for there is one!)
Of the unending, rhapsodic flow beside us (you and I)
Who is hurrying home to write something astonishing.

320.

After a morning spent making a start writing a tedious official
  autobiography,
He ventures out into the garden for a fresh bout of rest and
  replenishment.
On an impulse, he keeps walking, and strolls off down the narrow
  lane beyond.
Fifteen days later, he strolls back in, closing the gate pensively behind
  him.

321.

So, let us stand together here, at this ordinary street corner,
And try to identify which is the passer-by
Of the unending, spasmodic flow beside us – it shouldn't take too
  long –
Who has had enough of life, but can't yet quite manage to die.

322.

Ignoring as a vulgar and trivial matter the current fighting within
  their city,
For the whole afternoon the two greatly esteemed sages contend in
  elevated debate
On the question of whether Life and Death do really as such exist.
Alas, at the crucial point of their argument, their pavilion suffers a
  direct hit.

323.

Or let us stand together, at this ordinary street corner here,
And fail to identify which is the passer-by
Of the unending, ambivalent flow beside us
Who is bringing most torture into another person's life.

324.
On Visiting My Aunt, the retired Imperial Concubine, Swaying Blossom,
At her charming Hillside Retreat, near the Pearl Breath of Spring Lake,
To congratulate her on reaching her 82nd Birthday, and (alas!) finding her
    absent.
Oh, no! Not again! This is all I bloody need! Typical! How too
    bloody typical!

325.
The trees momentarily frame him as he stands on the path.
But the moment passes, as usual, and he has disappeared –
Having taken perhaps the most important decision of his entire life.
Not much later, he comes back into sight, now heading in the
    opposite direction.

326.
A cluster of rocks deep in the mass of trees.
Do the roots and trunks slowly, with each passing year,
Grow round them and past them and over them and into them and
    through them?
I suspect they must do. Oh, look! There's someone else running away!

327. *Opera Scene: 'The Pragmatic Lover of Nature'*
'A crumbling, rock-strewn gully among the trees near here
Has provided me with the perfect hiding-place throughout my life
For the rotted, rotten and rotting heads of various local nonentities
Who have caused me so much needless disappointment and injury.'

328. *Folksong*
'What? Does pure joy move these reeds?
Footsteps. Something like thunder slightly too near.
I thought for a moment that was a building over there. No?
These trees! Is it not? No? Art thou quite sure, my dying dear?'

78

329. *Historical Scene*
Gasping, he clings to the trunk of the wizened tree.
Surely he has managed to shake off his pursuers by now?
From just behind him, he hears a gentle, embarrassed cough.
Clearly, this cannot possibly be *another* bloody enemy?

330. *A Political Allegory*
'Towards noon, the wayfarer makes a startling discovery.
This new sort of tree is not really a sort of tree at all!
It is, in fact, something more resembling a large, carnivorous insect.
Not a very cheering thing to learn when deep in the heart of a forest,
     is it?'

331.
If they were to leave this curving path here,
And venture into the unmarked forest beyond,
What an astonishing ruin they might discover!
However, they are already *much* too late for their game.

332.
True, this pale, drawn, emaciated scholar
Sauntering calmly down a path through the forest
Will never write anything of the slightest importance. No.
But a deep, contented smile is playing about his lips, even so.

333.
This is the little bridge at the edge of the forest
Across which a wood-cutter will be walking, deep in thought, within
     ten minutes or so.
While over there, oddly enough, is a group of people politely arguing.
     Yes.
And here is the very spot where the bones will be found lying.

334.

A flutter of rooks deep in the mass of trees.

Do the rooks and trunks slowly, with each passing year,

Grow round them and past them and over them and into them and
through them?

Well, how could they possibly do so? (Oh, look! There's somebody
else running away!)

335.

When the complex point in dispute comes up once again during their
walk,

They cannot delay the settling of it even for a moment longer.

The two old scholars hurriedly disappear in among some trees –

From which one of them re-emerges triumphantly only a few minutes
later.

336.

Here we see this locality's celebrated and extremely ancient Tree Dance.

Once a decade, the natives ceremonially blindfold themselves

And attempt to skip and gambol their way clean through a thick,
swampy forest, without fatalities.

An old religious rite, obviously – which it is hardly for outsiders to sit
in judgement upon, is it?

337.

Towards noon, the wanderer makes a startling discovery.

No. This new sort of tree is not really a sort of tree at all!

Rather, it seems to be more like a close relative of something like a
deep-sea cucumber.

H'm. Clearly, he has taken, somewhere or other, a very wrong
turning indeed.

338. *Opera Scene: 'Under Mi Wu'*
'Has the resting monk noticed that the tree beside him has an orifice
    in it?
I would guess, from his relaxed behaviour, that he has not.
True – he may merely be (brilliantly) feigning indifference,
But I doubt it. After all, he's very perceptive. *And* he's a monk.'

339.
So, the old adage that one tree does not make a forest
Can be quite wrong, he contentedly thinks to himself,
Sitting out in his garden, with his back to an easeful trunk,
Facing a moss-covered wall almost directly against his feet.

340.
The picture is so old that it has faded almost to nothing.
There is only the slightest suggestion of a high wall and a few trees;
And a road winding away towards a fortunate house –
Very like the house, in fact, where the picture is itself hanging.

341.
A thin, empty road leads quietly up a hill.
Another turning that seems to know exactly where it's going.
Well: should he follow it up or shouldn't he?
Perhaps he should. Who knows? Perhaps, indeed, he should.

342.
A painful moment. Returning to his native village at last,
He discovers that the place has more or less entirely disappeared.
Pensively, he leans against one of the few remaining trees.
It breaks. And there's his whole past preserved right there inside it!
    (How did *that* happen!)

343.
There is his destination, at the top of the hill.
What a perfect moonlit night! If only there were
Still two or three more quiet valleys for him to negotiate!
Why did he not walk more slowly – even more slowly? Ah, well …

344.
A joyful moment. Returning at last to his native village,
He discovers that the place has almost entirely disappeared.
Contentedly, he urinates against one of the few remaining trees.
Yes. Such a strangely nostalgic thing for him to be doing!

345.
Can the Sage not see what effect his wayward thoughts are having
On the branch which waves so loosely above his meditation pavilion?
   No.
(Oh, let me not mislead you. They are having no effect at all.
No. The branches would still be performing those sardonic antics
   anyway.)

346.
After enjoying for a while the refreshing oscillation
Of a branch swaying just beyond the second-storey monastery window,
The visiting Abbot looks out – and discovers it is not attached to any
   single tree!
'You can't fool me!' he calls out to it. 'Listen, dear. You can't fool me!'

347. *Impromptu Wall Inscription*
'Yes. Remarkable how that one extremely long branch
Sweeps gently down to the surface of this dark, quiet lane.
I hope that all those who live hereabouts know of it and sufficiently
   admire it. Yes. Yes, I certainly do.
Hmm. On second thoughts – what am I talking about? I simply could
   not possibly care less about it, could I?'

348.

The official who used to live across the lane has moved to a new post;
And so the two rare old jade candlesticks which he had shared with a
　　helpful neighbour
Will never again be close; although, for night after night,
Their lights once flickered so near to each other among the same quiet
　　trees.

349.

Turmoil in the trees of the village lane
Of a brief storm that will never be seen again,
However the lights in the nearby houses dim or flare
In this normal moment's intensity of the air.

350. *An Inscription on the Other Side of the Wall*

'Remarkable how that single long branch from the blossoming
　　plum-tree
Sinks down almost to the surface of the dark quiet lane and runs all
　　the way along it.
I trust that those who live nearby know of it and admire it as much as
　　it deserves.
Unless, of course, they prefer to avoid this somewhat eerie
　　thoroughfare entirely.'

351.

An impressively tall skeleton is climbing a wall in the lane.
It stops at the top, and looks down into the garden.
A gay gentleman drinker w(e)arily returns its look –
Then shouts out: 'Go away!' (Which it does, absolutely mortified.)

352.

One could easily overlook this enchanting, sheltered house,
Hidden in the lea of a bigger house in the lane.
As one realises when one returns later, trying to find it again.
Where on earth has it gone? Somewhere around here, surely?

353.
The Master wanders, baffled, down a city lane,
Tenderly nursing some fresh abrasions on his torso.
Oh, why must some physical illusions always react so *violently*
When he points out to them, even very gently, that they *don't actually*
   exist?

354.
Remarkable how the long, long branch of that tree curves
And runs along just above the surface of the dark quiet lane.
I trust that all those who live here must know of it and admire it.
(Not that one quite needs to live here to know of it and admire it, of
   course.)

355.
Alas, this cultured city of artists and administrators
Has still not quite recovered from that hideous afternoon
When all the leading painters of sophisticated twigs
Were invited to a big, stone villa – which somehow then managed to
   burn down.

356.
On Visiting My Aunt, the retired Imperial Concubine, Swaying Blossom,
At her charming Hillside Retreat, near the Pearl Breath of Spring Lake,
To congratulate her on reaching her 85th Birthday, and (alas!) finding her absent
What? Where are you, you stupid old cow? Come on! *For God's sake!*
   This time we even had an effing appointment! I mean to say ...
   Two and a half more hours of my life *completely wasted*! You know?
   Orioles!

357. *Opera Scene: 'Not All Rumours Are Untrue'*
'Haven't you heard? The revered, ancient tree has somehow been
    chopped down during the night!'
'But this is just how the old prophecies foretell the fall of the dynasty!'
'Many of the guards, perhaps all too credulous, have taken to terrified
    flight. While, up on the roof,
The Crown Prince, with drunken bravado, is screaming: 'Frankly, my
    dear, I don't give a shite!'

358.
In the moonlight, on one of the smaller palace balconies,
Four elderly court ladies are doing a slow, dignified dance
For a blind diviner who is standing nearby, quite ostentatiously nude.
Yes. To be able to see the future, one must first 'get into the right
    mood'.

359. *An Inscription*
'We do not hear the noise of those who built this palace.
We do not hear the silence of the later (present) crowds.
No. We dodge falling debris, and think nobly of impermanence,
While the thin rain still manages to penetrate future roofs.'

360. *Thoughtful Folksong*
'Pulse after pulse of rain sweeps into the forest.
A hungry monkey scurries along a path.
A blind recluse, sighing, shelters against a tree.
Neither is in the least aware of you. Or, indeed, of me.'

361. *And Another*
'And now at last we have reached the untouched forest.
In all this wide, wild, unvariegated foliage
There is perhaps only a single human being wandering today.
Apart from you, of course. Hello. Who are you, by the way?'

362. *A Vanished Inscription*
'Where could I better live than beside these dull, uncorrupted lakes?
Even on those rare occasions when one does discover a new path,
It is never a path which leads to any excessively beguiling goal.
So then. Could there be a fitter place for burying one's worst mistakes?'

363. *Wanderer's Lovesong*
'This simple path leads towards nothing obvious.
But, as we have found it, we may as well follow it.
After all, we don't yet know it is going nowhere in particular, do we?
What? Really? Well ... darling ... I think you *might* have told me
   earlier. Why not?'

364.
Autumn. Sadness. A well-trodden path.
A half-ruined life lying against a wall.
A half-ruined life lying against a wall?
Yes. Yes: a half-ruined life lying against a wall.

365.
Thousands of bamboo plants along the river in Summer.
And only one man there among them in all that space.
If he is trying to hide, he has certainly chosen the right place.
But, quite possibly, he's not even trying to hide.

366.
The small, sheltered garden is almost hidden by an overhanging cliff.
If I were anywhere within it, I would not feel particularly safe.
In fact, even next door I don't feel particularly safe anyway.
However, at least I've been greatly heartened by a piece of very good
   news I received last night.

367. *A Political Allegory*
'Fences and leaves serve almost to hide the house.
He sits inside it, day after day, wrestling with his fears;
But he cannot prevent his memories from seeping out of his ears.
A truly terrible predicament for someone of such tender years!'

368.
Thousands of bamboo plants along a river in Autumn.
And five men there among them. Three of them singly,
And one tormented pairing. Or, some moments later,
Three of them singly, and a fourth singly too.

369.
Gloom is beginning to settle on the river-bank.
A grim-faced man riding a donkey hurries home.
A forlorn cry reverberates from the forest.
A forlorn echo reverberates in the forest.

370.
Clouds like long fingers seem to clutch at the horizon.
Among pine-trees, near the edge of a sudden cliff,
The grim-faced old rogue sits down for a moment's rest,
His own long fingers clenching and unclenching.

371. *An Almost Faded Inscription*
'I dreamt that the river here was in fact my pavilion
And that the clouds were the very water I was viewing.
What the sky beyond signified, I can no longer quite recall.
But then – what does the sky beyond ever quite signify?'

372. *A Slightly Less Natural Scene*
Land visible among the wisps of mist.
A flood of water pours from a cleft.
A tree leans out drunkenly from a rock-face.
The poetess falls off her seat, thoroughly pissed.

373. *A Political Allegory*
'Remarkable how one immensely long branch of this tree,
Although surely so heavy, maintains itself still in the air.
The trunk is not thick, nor the roots, seemingly, extensive.
We feel it simply ought not to be able to do that. And yet, it does ...'

374.
The scholar stands on a branch near the top of the old tree,
Glaring defiance at the presumably mythological presence
Which is lurking below in his garden, in the gloomy fading light,
Complaining about some gross improbability in his new work.

375.
The man of genius cools himself in the meditation pavilion
With a delicately painted fan, on which a young woman
Is playing in a garden in a posture strangely similar
To that which his silent wife has just taken up inside the house.

376.
Refreshed, the newly awakened, hyper-sophisticated philosopher
Is twitching his antennae about in a vegetable garden
As if trying to attract a likely mate. Yes. It seems
He has lately been paying far too much attention to his dreams.

377.

The two philosophers meeting as if by chance beside the stream
Again begin to discuss whether or not they really exist –
Before recalling how often they have already had such fruitless
    discussions.
Realising this, they laugh, and all three of them disappear back into
    the bushes together.

378.

The two or more philosophers sitting on a slight chine by the river,
After spending a few pleasant moments discussing chance and change,
Turn their attention to an immense chain hanging from the sky
    directly overhead.
Soon, they are forced (predictably enough!) to quite fiercely opposed
    conclusions.

379. *A Funerary Inscription*

'Although uncertain whether it was merely a troubled, chance or
    sentimental behest –
Or, in fact, a serious expression of his mature philosophy –
We have nonetheless placed above his grave this comparatively
    restrained image
Of his colleagues being devoured by ants – in accordance with his
    final request.'

380.

Empty room – empty room – empty room – empty room – empty
    room –
(The lower floor of the temple is at present quite unoccupied.)
Empty room – empty room – monk playing with himself – empty
    room –
(Actually ... the upper floor *should* also be empty just at the moment.)

381.

The first wife weeps as she hides on a veranda.

The third wife frowns tensely as she peeps through a gap in a fence.

Both are spying on the pair in the garden, each thinking: 'That should really be me!' –

While the second wife, down there with him, wishes [s]he were somewhere else.

382.

After hearing his youngest daughter's anguished confession of her latest fault,

The wise, old retired magistrate raised her from her knees, smiled kindly, and said:

'No mere human misjudgement could ever alienate me from you, my darling, my prop, my staff and my stay.'

Unfortunately, his irate wife then knocked her senseless with a substantial rosewood tray.

383.

The Northern Wing phrase for, 'May I humbly enquire after your esteemed health and family?'

Is treacherously similar in sound to how, in Southern Wing, one might perhaps choose to observe:

'I long to inhale deeply at all your wife's various gorgeous and invigorating orifices.'

Yes. One must take great care with personal enquiries in the border country.

384. *Upper-Class Drinking Song*
'The top of the hill is up at the top, whereas the bottom is down at
  the bottom.

Speaking of which: what is your charming young lady wife doing this
  morning?

Let me try to guess. Perhaps pretending to be visiting her sister, while
  in fact having wild, raw sex with her cretinous brother-in-law?
  Oh –

But I was forgetting. You keep no secrets from each other, do you,
  Your Excellency?'

385. *Drinking Song*
'What I like most about spring is my wife's rear end.

What I like most about summer is my wife's backside.

What I like most about autumn is my wife's arse.

What I like most about winter is – oh God! No! God! She's gone and
  left me! Why, ye Gods? Why? Why?'

386. *Drinking Song*
'Bums! *(With an extremely crude gesture.)*

Bums! *(With an appreciably less crude gesture.)*

Bums! *(With a really rather sensitive gesture, all things considered.)*

Oh, I'm terribly sorry. I probably ought to have said "nates".'

387.
Good heavens – this latest addition to his porcelain collection,

Now that he looks more closely at its subtle, refined construction,

Surely bears a remarkable resemblance to his own dear lady wife's jade
  store?

Yes. He picks it up and sidles into the little room next door.

388.
The old scholar stands astonished at a corner of his garden wall.
Since last he was there, it seems, the mosses and lichens
Have re-combined and have conspired to form the austere classical
    term for the *'pudendum muliebre'*.
Not that *all* the dictionaries quite agree on this one, of course.

389. *From a Scholarly Letter of Apology*
'Esteemed Sir, that unforgettable morning when you at last allowed
    me to inspect your world-famous collection of antique jades
Followed hard upon the very night when, after a prolonged period of
    tears, entreaty and disputation,
My perhaps somewhat over-fastidious new young wife finally allowed
    me to admire her *ori, tep, ava, nu, denpa, eh* AND *la* in a leisurely
    manner by subdued and tasteful candlelight.
I therefore trust you will accept that I was in fact, given the particular
    circumstances then obtaining, quite astonishingly enthusiastic.
    Thank you.'

390.
Good heavens – that old bowl lying neglected among his ever-
    extending collection –
Now that he looks more closely at its subtle and refined construction –
Surely it bears a more than fleeting resemblance to one of his late first
    wife's jade dorbits?
Hmm. Quickly, he picks it up, kisses it, and shoves it safe into his own
    'very special' cupboard.

391.
Hmm. The fan his vapid old neighbour is waving languorously about
Has, painted on it, a landscape which, at one particular angle,
Reminds him a great deal of a certain private aspect of his rather plain
    wife next door. H'm.
Soon he makes an excuse and leaves early, blaming the mounting heat.

392.

The official wakes up and sighs. Of course; of course.

In this cramped temporary accommodation, again,

He is forced to sleep in a single bed with all three of his wives at once.

All right. Whose hand is holding the incomparable jade pendant *this*
time?

393.

The ancient eunuch cools himself in his meditation pavilion

With a delicately painted fan, on which a young woman

Is lying dully in a garden in a posture strangely similar

To that which his own mother often assumed in the weeks before his
birth.

394.

The old connoisseur sits alone in his study, again almost weeping.

By now the room must contain several dozen exquisite jugs, urns and
vases —

Inside some of which lie the dust of various dead colleagues and friends.

Of course, there were one or two he much preferred to the others.

395.

One of this magnificent pair of ornate, encrusted daggers

Is lain in a place of honour in the retired general's hallway —

Even as a smiling eunuch, on a slow evening in the Palace,

Is, alas, putting its mate to an unsavoury, almost repellent, use.

396.

His cries of pain and confusion are all the more unexpected

In that, for the past few years, the waylaid and bleeding traveller

Has increasingly inclined to the view that all that exists is mere illusion.

But — possibly this illusion thing is part of the illusion too? (*Eh?*)

397. *A Second Last Poem*

'Just as I was so enjoying timelessness in the nearby lane yet again,
I collapsed here on this very spot and died – of a heart attack,
    presumably –
Surviving only for long enough to scribble down these three
    inadequate lines.
But, alas, a fourth and concluding one is still needed … Yes … Rather
    typical that …

398. *Embittered Traveller's Song*

'It seemed to me that I might possibly be riding the wrong animal.
And then I thought: well, yes – of course I am! Of course!
After all, everyone on earth is in fact riding the wrong animal.
Yes. They're usually even the wrong bloody animal themselves, are
    they not?'

399.

On Visiting My Aunt, the retired Imperial Concubine, Swaying Blossom,
At her charming Hillside Retreat, near the Pearl Breath of Spring Lake,
To congratulate her on reaching her 87th Birthday, and (alas!) finding her
    absent.

Right. Fine – I hope you're happy, you old bitch! I just hope you're
    very happy! My mother always *did* say you were a complete tart,
    you know. And, by God, she was right! Indeed she was. Yes.
    Oriolas! (Is that the right word?)

400.

Furtively, the Sage opens the top of his head.
He takes out the ultimate secret of the universe,
Fondles it, kisses it – then puts it back inside.
Yes. A brief moment of quiet, surely forgivable pride!

Book Five: The Harsh Fields of the Inkslab

401.
'It is so important ...
Not to overhear what ...
What the whole universe ...
Is not in fact saying ...'

402.
For seventeen full years, the Sage has talked to no-one –
Following his vow to remain completely silent
Until he discovers the secret of the universe.
But, five seconds ago, he made a brief remark to himself. [*Fool!*]

403.
Inside the rented room, three labourers are arguing.
Beyond the door, two women are standing silent,
Anxiously awaiting the result of this latest dispute.
Nearly everyone there is thinking, 'Please don't let it be me!'

404.
Disciples follow every twist and turn in the fierce debate
Of the rival religious leaders, arguing forcefully and fluently.
They cry out at every great new insight revealed to them.
They gasp whenever a skull is thumped with more than usual weight.

405.

A few savants, inspecting a fine, newly discovered ancient sculpture
Of a legendary being – is it? – who somehow by dying gave birth
To the entire cosmos, eventually throw off all mean-spirited restraint,
And defend their various interpretations in a fair and open fist-fight.

406.

Inside the room, two scholars argue passionately –
While, just beyond them, two maids are standing, silent,
Secretly listening, intrigued by what they can hear.
Soon, the scholars themselves are intrigued by scuffling sounds behind
    the door.

407.

This is obviously a calm, well-ordered scholar's private retreat.
This is where one might very well expect to find a person
Who would happily consecrate his entire life to the pursuit of truth,
    knowledge and social justice.
Unfortunately, the place has been completely abandoned for the last
    fifteen years at least.

408.

If the great poet is at present in his garden,
He is certainly not in the chaste, carefully tended nearer portion of it.
Perhaps he is hidden somewhere among the deep blooms by the wall?
(One assumes those charming squeals are coming from the
    neighbour's summer-house?)

409. *A Polished Rebuke*

'Esteemed Sir, I made a considerable detour to visit you in your out-
   of-the-way villa here.

I knocked at the door again and again, but no-one ever answered.

All I could hear, eventually, was someone giggling and a rough voice
   saying, "Ssshh!"

I merely leave you this note, Sir, lest the ignorance of these puzzling
   phenomena might in any way prove unrewarding to you (*plural*).'

410.

On Visiting My Aunt, the retired Imperial Concubine, Swaying Blossom,
At her charming Hillside Retreat, near the Pearl Breath of Spring Lake,
To congratulate her on reaching her 88th Birthday, and (alas!*) finding her absent.*

Oh, arseholes! Help! This time they will definitely kill me if I don't
   repay them! Help! Help! I'm being followed! Help!

411. *Written on the Back Wall*

'After a journey of several weeks, seeking out your spiritual guidance,

I arrived here at *The Hermitage of Sage and Sacred Contemplation* –

To discover that you had just been arrested for grossly insulting an
   earlier, unwanted visitor.

Oh, if only I had not dallied for quite so long in my insignificant
   approach!'

412.

Empty room – empty room – empty room – empty room – empty
   room –

(The lower floor of the temple is unoccupied at present.)

Empty room – empty room – two monks playing with themselves –
   empty room –

(H'm. The spiritual retreat has evidently ended rather sooner than
   anticipated.)

413.
A Goddess with five, six or seven arms sits weeping just outside the
    Great Temple gates.
She came down to earth, so young, eager and willing to help men,
But all they seem to want to do is discuss how she prefers to masturbate.
Still. Who is to say that has *nothing whatever* to do with the spiritual life?

414.
Perplexed monks gather around the guest itinerant instructor
Who is demonstrating a means of clapping using only one hand.
They clearly suspect that trickery must be involved here somewhere –
    but where?
I mean to say, that can't be his *testicles* doing that ... can it?

415.
Such a surprise, yes, when by this calm, contemplative temple-pond,
To notice six golden carp which – well, in fact, even five of them
Would already have been the – erm – let's see – or only four, perhaps?
So. Right. Yes. Well ... a lovely peaceful spot anyway.

416.
Just then, two half-naked monks are seen on the very roof of the
    women's quarters!
The audience reacts to this new twist with considerable discomfiture.
Indeed, within an hour, an unsophisticated mob has burned the entire
    theatre down to the ground.
(Yes. Sudden experiments with realism can at times be *infinitely* risky.)

417.
Leaping about brandishing a spear, the over-enthusiastic actor
Inadvertently slices off most of his private parts.
The audience applauds madly at this unusually convincing touch.
So. At least this particular sacrifice for art *was* appreciated. (Which is
    always something.)

418.

The audience gasps with delight at the astonishing denouement.
It turns out that the wise old woman is the gay hero's long-lost
    grandfather!
While his loyal wife is really the good blackmailer's own favourite son!
So there we are. As it turns out, a little something for everyone.

419.

The actor reappears, this time wearing the very rare mask
Which indicates that he is a rich, good-humoured eccentric
Who is much given to forcing money, unsolicited, onto casual
    passers-by.
Inadvertently, the cognoscenti in the audience press ever so slightly
    forward.

420.

On Visiting My Aunt, the retired Imperial Concubine, Swaying Blossom,
At her charming Hillside Retreat, near the Pearl Breath of Spring Lake,
To congratulate her on reaching her 90th Birthday, and (alas!) finding her absent.
What? Again? Oh, I'll get you for this yet, you old skinflint, just you
    wait! (Yes. And I always *did* love you, you know!) But no more.
    No. Not in a million years! Never! (Was it maybe something I
    said?) (Or if not that, then what? Eh? Do tell me!) Why won't you
    even tell me? Eh? Please! Anyway I won't be coming back here
    again – have no fear of that. No. This is definitely the last time.
    Yes. Quite definitely. Yes …

421. *A Political Allegory*

'A small road leads under a bridge to a hill suburb,
Considered to be by far the most fashionable area of town.
A blind man with blood newly pouring from his nose
Is standing at the street corner, extremely disenchanted.'

422.

There will never be such an afternoon for him again.
He stops on the path, as he has so often done before,
To watch someone working in an ordinary garden nearby.
Perhaps their eyes even meet – but, this time, it has very little
    significance.

423.

The old official picks up and gently shakes a tiny box
Containing one-off earrings given to him by various women
Whose lives never approached to within even a day's journey of each
    other.
He smiles at the utterly wonderful disharmony it all makes.

424.

This venerable old instrument, shaped curiously like a scrotum,
Has such a weak sound and inadequate range
That its use would surely have died out long ago
Had very many court ladies not taken it so to their hearts.

425.

The old sage sits in the narrow garden, next to a group of women
Who are performing music for him, using all eight classical sounds:
Silk, bamboo, metal, stone, wood, leather, gourds and earthenware.
And there's sometimes even a voice too. (A sort of joyful cry.)

426.

Thousands of bamboo plants along a river in autumn –
Some five men there among them. Three of them singly
And one troubled group of two. Or, some moments later,
Just one of them singly. (Hello? What happened *there*?)

427.
The doctor jolts along in a cart all morning, crosses
A small river, stops, and has a rough but adequate meal.
He rests for a good while; then, in the afternoon,
He continues to jolt along in a cart for a few hours more.

428.
Such a joy – to have found a place where the old religion survives!
Enchanted, the weary traveller finishes off the rich, nourishing, sacred
    brew.
Then, with a thankful sigh, he puts the cleared bowl back down
Onto the still flowing numen of the withering priestess.

429.
The astronomer stands in his garden, gazing up at the stars.
His smiling wife looks down at him from a sheltered balcony.
Behind her, kneels a monk, pressing against her heavenly rear end.
Ah! This eternal, sad, needless conflict between science and religion!

430. *Sent with a Gift*
'Today I send you this clutch of fresh, white, beautifully-petalled
    peonies,
Hoping thereby to share my delight in them with you, Madam;
Since you did not turn up yesterday evening, despite all your golden,
    glowing promises.
And I was therefore unable to perform certain highly appropriate
    flowing movements with them.'

431.
The Western Huang phrase for 'It rather looks like rain, doesn't it?'
Is almost identical in sound to the Eastern Huang phrase which means,
'I greatly desire, Your Eminence, to watch you relieve yourself among
    my rare prize peonies.'
(Ah! Since ancient times, the weather has caused much tension in
    Huang!)

432.
This rare character seems to mean, 'The subtle misfortune
Of owning two large and beautiful estates, many miles apart,
Each of which one adores – especially when in the other.' Yes.
Some dictionaries also give 'underwear' – which must surely be wrong?

433. *Opera Scene: 'Su Shi, the Patriotic Scholar'*
'When we learn that the more exhaustive classical dictionaries
Give some fifty-odd different characters for the expression 'to defecate'
We may perhaps catch a glimpse of just how crucial the profession of
  politics –
Er, sorry, no – of *agriculture* is, in this great Empire of ours.'

434. *A Seasonal Note*
'Is any of our characters more beautiful than "Autumn"?
Who can ever look at it without instantly imagining
A couple lying together, talking quietly in a bed,
About the rare, unsteady music they can hear inside their head?'

435.
On Visiting My Aunt, the retired Imperial Concubine, Swaying Blossom,
At her charming Hillside Retreat, near the Pearl Breath of Spring Lake,
To congratulate her on reaching her 91st Birthday, and (alas!) finding her absent.
Look – I can just tell you're hiding behind the bed, you old bitch! Do
  you think I don't *know* that? Listen to me. THERE IS NOTHING
  TO BE AFRAID OF. COME OUT AT ONCE! (No. That wasn't
  really *me* last time by the way.) Hello?

436. *Second-Last Chapter of a Novel*
After hearing his eldest daughter's tearful confession of guilt,
The retired, elderly magistrate raised her from her knees, smiled, and
  said:
'Small cause for worry, my darling. We can cope. We can always cope.'
Then he went off into the garden, to look for a reliable rope.

437.
For forty-seven years he has spent nearly every available free moment
Sitting in his library, copying out significant and improving extracts
     from the Classics,
Intending at some later point to return to them, reread them, and
     learn from them the deepest secrets of the human heart.
But – yes. That is his body now hanging from a rope in the corner.

438. *Sketch for an Epitaph*
'The lanes of his native province will seem emptier to us now,
Or the feverish night the darker for his so untypical absence.
And as for his need to force inferiors down into rank insanity,
Well, for that matter, what is sanity anyway? Eh? Oh, look! Another
     beaver!'

439. *A Parting Inscription*
'On reaching your spare cottage, dear Sir, I learned that you had lately
     died.
Hearing which I turned away, sadly, carrying back my now
     superfluous gifts.
So many things, I think, which you would have greatly liked to have.
     But no matter.
As a mark of my utmost respect for you, old friend, I shall simply keep
     them.'

440.
On Visiting My Aunt, the retired Imperial Concubine, Swaying Blossom,
At her charming Hillside Retreat, near the Pearl Breath of Spring Lake,
To congratulate her on reaching her 92nd Birthday, and (alas!) finding her
     absent.
All right! All right! But couldn't you at least leave me *half* of it?

441.
On the day after the death of the austere district magistrate,
A thick folder of secret, personal poems is discovered –
Including many which mention the exciting moles of some
    unidentified female acquaintance[s].
That night, all the family men who knew him are haunted by much
    the same thought.

442. *A Note Attached to the Bequest*
'Since you, my heirs, have (I assume) at last found this rich, proud cache
Of precious insignia of office, learn then that each one of them
Has been inserted at least once (gently enough, let us hope) into some
    amused female or other's delicate and yet so strangely familiar
    interior.
But now your revered though unmarried ancestor leaves them, fairly
    respectfully, to your august trust. (*Orioles!)'*

443.
The great general sits fretting in his favourite room –
A study adorned with several superb large vases.
You would hardly believe what there is inside several of those vases.
[Well, I don't believe it either – and I carried them in myself!]

444. *From 'An Allegory on Transience'*
'The old traditional doctor who thought to extend his life organically
By having his new wife sit on his face for most of the morning
Has, she discovers to her dismay, passed away in the last few minutes.
However, his final expression at least to some extent does soften the
    blow.'

445.

Since being informed by his doctor that he had at most a year to live,
The great thinker has spent almost all his time in the pleasure-quarters,
Sniffing away at select apertures while strength and money might last.
    Yes.
All but one of his greatest achievements now lie firmly in the past.

446.

Many are aghast at the rumour now sweeping through Heaven.
Can it be true that there is another Paradise not so very far away?
But this is intolerable! Why are we not there? Well?
Who cares how happy they are? Well? Why are *we* not there?

447.

As the two of them walked in silence down the quiet city lane,
They met a third person, whom they did not recognise
Even though they knew him slightly – for the man had recently died.
Nor did he even say the briefest 'Hello!' to them as he hurried past.

448.

In his tent, before the battle, in the last hours of the night,
The General scrupulously briefs his ingenious Second-in-Command,
Heroically overlooking the fact that he died in the previous fight.
Yes. But apart from that single oversight, the preparations were
    flawless.

449.

Well, this man here clearly understands the whole Cosmos!
We can tell that from the calmness with which he ignores
The *chic* birds defecating upon him from the ostensibly higher branches.
Yes. They're non-existent too. Yet another dead giveaway ...

450. *To the Tune of 'Simultaneous Indulgence in Three of Life's Greatest Joys'*
'Aha! At last! Here comes the Third Mandarin now! What can have
   kept him? Hello!
He'll certainly put an end to all this immature, dualistic farfing about.
What? Oh no! Look! Oh, no! He's just fallen into an open sewer!
   How did *that* happen?
What tough luck! Yes. Oh, well. The world, alas, would now seem to
   be at least one Mandarin fewer!'

451.
Meanwhile, on another part of the same scroll,
The disgraced twin who, from mere chagrin, flung himself right off
   the overhang,
Is trudging yet again up the path towards the summit
With an unexpected expression of baffled joy on his face.

452.
Such mist and rain on the narrow path down the wooded slope!
Someone could easily have reached that fine, isolated house
Before the girl walking in the garden would catch sight of him.
Or her, of course. (If that him now by the gate?)

453. *Mixed Reflections Improvised at Innumerable Interior Points*
Evening – across the broad river, mist and roofs.
Morning – across the broad river, brightness and roofs.
A strangely lucid place, that dreams should so evaporate here!
But, after all, life evaporates here too, does it not?

454.

On Visiting My Aunt, the retired Imperial Concubine, Swaying Blossom,
At her charming Hillside Retreat, near the Pearl Breath of Spring Lake,
To congratulate her on reaching her 94th Birthday, and (alas!) finding her absent.
Look, Auntie; I'm getting on. I now have twin daughters. Things cost
    money, don't they? Let's try to be civilised, mature, adult human
    beings about this, eh? What do you say? Oh – and many happy
    returns too, you dear old darling! Mwah! Mwah!

455.

Meanwhile, on another part of the same va[r]nished screen,
The God who, for some reason or other, flung himself off the
    mountain-top,
Is trudging up the harsh path towards the summit again
With an ever more grimly resolute expression on his [invisible] face.

456.

The two mages have travelled together for almost an entire week.
Now they approach the ferry-path where they must at last part.
At such a fraught moment, what can each possibly say?
(Even so, it's fairly surprising that all of them have started to squeak.)

457.

The immense shadow does not worry them in the slightest,
Even though they have travelled for an entire day within it.
After all, it is only yet another metaphor for life, is it not?
Indeed – the landscape hereabouts seems to consist of little else.

458.

Alas, the mountain view is not at its best in this weather.
Its attractions are somewhat obscured by a thin, mean-minded mist.
Nonetheless, one can still hear, off somewhere in the distance,
Yet more fascinating sounds of a fine day just ceasing to exist.

459. *A Note on Departing*
'Almost a week has passed since I first came to this inn,
Accidentally discovered during a ramble among the hills.
And now, just as I leave, I hear high laughter not far above me,
Truly, the perfect sound with which such visits should begin!'

460.
Meanwhile, on another part of the same extended scroll,
The old cripple who somehow toppled over into a precipice
Is walking at great speed up a path towards the summit
With a warped, merciless smile on his eerily youthful face.

461.
On Visiting My Aunt, the retired Imperial Concubine, Swaying Blossom,
At her charming Hillside Retreat, near the Pearl Breath of Spring Lake,
To congratulate her on reaching her 95th Birthday, and (alas!) finding her absent.
I won't be back, you know! The doctors tell me I'm critically ill. But
    I dare say that doesn't worry you in the slightest, does it? (Huh. I
    suppose you *do* know it's raining, don't you?)

462.
For most of the time, we forget how high up we are,
The land slopes so gently; crevasses
Appear near our feet in moments of forgetfulness –
As, in other places, do negligently discarded twigs.

463. *Lines Written in a Viewing Tower*
'On evenings of such space, viewed from such high
Pavilions, it becomes almost unbearably obvious
That I could fly away from here, if I merely wanted to fly.
Yes. I'll make up my mind in a minute or so – and then go!'

464. *A Political Allegory*
'Sire, the heron looks up, sees another heron fly
Far overhead, and wishes for an instant
That it could do likewise; before recalling, with rare discernment,
That it can, and rising wondrously even higher into the skies.'

465. *A Guarded Prophecy*
'The royal bird leaps without warning into the sky.
The lonely branch whimpers a few times, then subsides.
The leaves whisper conspiratorially among themselves.
As if wishing they too could do that, and therefore not die.'

466. *[Another Twenty]*
The huge birds appear on the horizon again.
In the border city, people stop and stare,
Wondering whether, today, they will dare come any nearer.
But they will fly off one time more, to the liar in his lair.

[*Alternative last line*:
But they will fly off one more time, and give the sky a tear.
Vel:
But they will fly off two more times, like the incestuous royal pair.
Vel:
But they will fly off three more times, terrifying the great air.
Vel:
But they will fly off four more times, until they form a square.
Vel:
But they will fly off five more times, with energy to spare.
Vel:
But they will fly off six more times, causing the sect much despair.
Vel:
But they will fly off seven more times, until the heavens are bare.
Vel:
But they will fly off eight more times, [p]ending the great affair.
Vel:
But they will fly off nine more times, with great harm to fine underwear.

Vel:

But they will fly off ten more times, till they recognise the air.

    [*Quaere*: 'heir'?]

Vel:

But they will fly off eleven more times, before the Year of the Hair.

    [*Quaere*: 'Hare'? (*Quaere*: 'Heir'?)]

Vel:

But they will fly off twelve more times, before vanishing in mid-air.

Vel:

But they will fly off thirteen more times – which does seem rather
    unfair.

Vel:

But they will fly off fourteen more times, [*madly / gladly / sadly*] badly
    the worse for wear.

Vel:

But they will fly off fifteen more times, suspecting a foul snare.

Vel:

But they will fly off sixteen more times, and make a royal stare.

Vel:

But they will fly off seventeen more times, and quack a royal stair.

    [*Eh?* 'Quake'? 'Crack'?]

Vel:

But they will fly off eighteen more times, and make a loyal swear.

Vel:

But they will fly off nineteen more times, cracking all the earthenware.

Vel:

But they will fly off twenty more times, while we amen[d] the prayer.

Vel:

But they will fly off twenty-one more times, as far as one is aware.]

467. *Indicted While Drunk at the Willow Bank Palace Palisade*

'How comforting it is, that we should drink here for centuries,

And that butterflies should veer through us for a good few centuries
    more.

I [shall] turn round to ask you something, but you have already departed.

So, instead, I watch the new leaves waver for another ten seconds or
    two.'

468. *Drinking Song*

'Both our [b]old scholar-companions are admiring the rolled-out
    sunset,

Neglecting the long, wise scroll that lies wide-open before them.

Now is our chance, my golden goddess – oh, ignore them! Just ignore
    them!

High time to do something unworthy among all this ancient wisdom!'

469. *Drinking Song*

'Oh, grant us a glimpse of thy *ton gue* (dear!) while the wild geese fly
    on by!

For everyone else will be watching – (cretins!) – the wild geese
    highing by.

But the sky is only the sky. The trees are only the trees.

And the earth is a mere piece of your necklace, floating free in the
    breeze.'

470.

That ridiculously drunk gentleman over there, face-down in the mud,

Is in fact directly descended from a very great figure indeed.

A leading general, was it? Or perhaps a magnificent poet? – But, no.

I forget precisely what sort of a gross disappointment he is.

471. *A Deep Drinking Song*

'Clearing the garden of debris after the previous evening's civilised
    party,

The servants find a dead body. Evidently not someone important.

Indeed, absolutely no-one seems to know whose body it is.

But then – do we know who *anyone* is, really? Cheers!'

472.

The dead-looking body lies in the charming city garden.

That noise must be the clamour of ordinary insects.

That scent is largely the scent of ordinary flowers.

The gate swings slowly open – very slowly – then swings back shut.

473. *Abendstimmung in Ku Ling*
A man is quietly walking across a bridge.
A dog sniffs about inside a nearby gate.
Another day out of thousands – for millions – draws to a normal close.
Yes. I dare say we must all have had at least one or two of those.

474.
Look! The dog arrives suddenly at the open door –
To be greeted by joyful shouts of recognition.
In appearance, it is still pretty much as cute as it was before.
(And it takes good care not to betray the least sign of ambition.)

475. *Perhaps a Familiar Theme*
A dirty dog strolls through the Palace, much disorientated and
Bemused that he should now be sole ruler of the great land of Cathay.
There is so much about this whole business which he cannot quite
    understand.
But then – how much does *any* ruler ever quite understand *really*?

476.
Over half the women in the palace are now wearing dog-collars.
What seemed such a curious occurrence back at the start of the
    Dynasty
Is now more and more being taken utterly for granted.
Ah – how insidiously the fine old values are supplanted!

477.
In the moonlight, on one of the larger palace balconies,
Various stately dames have embarked on a most unseemly *tan go*
For a group sitting nearby, who are all grinning broadly and egging
    them on.
(Were they not in such sacred robes, one would, frankly, be somewhat
    concerned.)

478.

Almost every week for twenty years, she has been brought to the Palace
To perform alone an artistic dance for a bigwig she has never seen.
Now, on her last morning, she finishes her show and waits.
But once more she is dismissed without a word from behind the screen.

479.

The lady can probably see him through a fissure in the panelled screen
From behind which the visiting Abbot listens to her cultured, delicate
    voice –
But he himself has not the slightest idea of her appearance –
Except for that single queer glimpse, years ago, of something almost
    obscene.

480.

On Visiting My Aunt, the retired Imperial Concubine, Swaying Blossom,
At her charming Hillside Retreat, near the Pearl Breath of Spring Lake,
To congratulate her on reaching her 98th Birthday, and (alas!) finding her absent.
Oh, for God's sake! Flames, flames, flames, flames, flames! Must I, so
    to speak, spell everything out?

481. *A Political Prophecy*
'A skeletal man lies at the side-entrance to a monastery,
With insufficient energy left to shout for help.
Had not a little charmer happened to slip through that door the next
    morning,
He might well have starved to death. Which, in fact, he does anyway.'

482.

The beggar, having persevered through three wide provinces,
Is now standing, with increasing mystification,
In a small, walled sunlit garden, seemingly devoid of doors.
Dreaming? Naked? Dead? What? Or merely fading away?

483.
A window out of which no-one ever looks.
A balcony onto which no-one ever steps.
Even the sunlight seems to have lost its way.
And all the pronouns fail, except for 'they'.
[For it cannot reach the edges of this particular Cathay.]

484. *Lines Inscribed in a Previous House*
'Walking in a quiet garden, searching for enlightenment
And then giving up the search for enlightenment
Is itself enlightenment enough. And thus, undisturbed,
One walks out the morning up and down the hushed path until
   lunchtime.'

485.
A somnolent stretch of water somewhere or other.
A leaf or two dips into the river.
A hand or two lets the flow trickle against it (or them).
A few more reflections startle the dull sky and then disappear.

486.
Thousands of bamboo plants along a river in autumn.
And four men there among them. A pair of them alone,
And one group of two. Or, a moment later – what?
Yes. Perhaps only a scattered handful of pulses in the water.

487.
A breeze – an empty bench – water descending –
Silence – footsteps – silence – water descending –
A few last rustling leaves – water descending –
Stillness – coolness – water descending – night.

488.
Thousands of bamboo plants along a river in autumn.
And nobody there among them. (None that we know of at least.)
And, indeed, why should anyone be there just at the moment?
No, the water is *always* making that cruel, disdainful, draining sound.

489.
He hides among the shrubs.
Yellow; red; green; black.
Are birds more fortunate than this?
A blade thrusting, hacking.

490. *An Expository Note*
'The symbolism of this denuded plum-tree,
Growing on the very rim of a cliff, beside
A broken bridge, should be indisputably obvious.
If not, the severed ear nearby may help to clarify matters.'

491. *A Traveller's Inscription*
'I fear that this small bridge over an irregular inlet
Links one irrelevant point with yet another irrelevant point
In the time-honoured manner of the best old, rural bridges.
But I'll find the right place hereabout eventually, I suppose.'

492.
The disturbed scholar awakes from his disturbing dream.
He lights his candle, and looks round hesitantly.
What is the source of that slight but insistent sound?
What? No! Is it really all only a wooden symbol?

493. *The Badly Received Impromptu*

'By this celebrated, remote, immensely thundering waterfall,
One may, even while in the selectest company,
Let rip a fart, assured that it will always go unheard.
And as for the smell – well, no doubt Nature can always cover that too.'

494. *Drinking Song*

'Once, out in the far west, I saw a yak which had almost human ears.
And I remembered instantly how, long ago in my Ka Lou years,
I had seen a freak in a hectic street whose ears were like those of a
    yak.'
(*Chorus*.) 'My father said he had very probably been unsuccessful in
    business.'

495.

And then the ancient sage rode off on the water buffalo
And was never seen again. Except for the rare occasions
When he *was* seen again. And even at those choice moments
No-one *quite* saw him. Though they sometimes did smell the buffalo.

496.

Whereat the Master rode up the sacred eastern slope
On his trusty steed, and, when he had reached the top,
An otherworldly being manifested itself at his side,
Pushed him off, stole the beast, and wafted invisibly away.

497.

After thirty-seven years of blameless living in a hut beside the town
    wall,
One morning the virtuous old recluse is discovered to have gone
    missing.
Likewise missing are both spinster sisters of the newly arrived Court
    Historian.
(Who is even now 'recalibrating' his previous view that *Coincidence
    Rules All*.)

498. *On Forgetting the Unforgettable*
'This is the thirty-ninth monastery I have now entered
In search of the ultimate spiritual enlightenment.
The sort I had, in fact – though briefly – during the very first hours of
  my journey!
(Oh, if only I could still remember what that overwhelming insight
  was!)'

499. *A Topographical Note*
'This small road is a mere swamp of churned mud,
Though it leads to the abode of the greatest thinker who has lived
  hereabouts for centuries.
(Yes. I do still wonder what he might be doing at this present moment.)
[Still. I dare say it's hardly worthwhile going all the way up there just
  to find out?]'

500.
On Visiting My Aunt, the retired Imperial Concubine, Swaying Blossom,
At her charming Hillside Retreat, to congratulate her on finally reaching her
  100th Birthday
And learning (alas!) that she had in fact died very shortly after I last met her.
Tragic news, of course. Tragic. Yes. But, really – couldn't someone
  have thought to tell me about this a bit earlier? No? Not even a
  whisper? A rumour? (I mean to say. Now, apart from anything
  else, I'll have to *pay my own way back*.)

501.
Every year, on the assumed anniversary of his death,
A pair of mandarins meet here in this fine but rather out-of-the-way
  wineshop,
To remember the dear friend who was once such a vital part of the
  wild, bright, incomparable trio of their youth. Yes.
H'm. (In fact, he's actually just upstairs, still pretty much alive.)